D1806005

Clarkson Gray,

AND OTHER POEMS.

BY

MRS JAMES MORTON.

SECOND EDITION.

Illustrated.

LONDON: HOULSTON & WRIGHT.   EDINBURGH: JOHN MENZIES.
GLASGOW: PORTEOUS BROTHERS.
1867.

280. m. 124.

This scarce antiquarian book is included in our special *Legacy Reprint Series*. In the interest of creating a more extensive selection of rare historical book reprints, we have chosen to reproduce this title even though it may possibly have occasional imperfections such as missing and blurred pages, missing text, poor pictures, markings, dark backgrounds and other reproduction issues beyond our control. Because this work is culturally important, we have made it available as a part of our commitment to protecting, preserving and promoting the world's literature.

FRONTISPIECE.

—page?

TO THE READER.

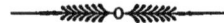

To paint a picture was my fond desire,
To Human Nature did my soul aspire;
But could I write till Nature's latest sun,
I yet would leave a picture but begun.

Yours respectfully,

JESSIE D. M. MORTON.

BLAIR COTTAGE, OAKLEY.

CONTENTS.

LIST OF ILLUSTRATIONS.

CLARKSON GRAY.

THINK not that castes exist but with the great,
They mark the lowest rank of man's estate ;
There, too, the base one of an ill report
Can shun the fellows of a baser sort,
And gems the brightest that adorn our kind
Among the poorest of the poor you'll find,
For generations their high castes can claim
The fair escutcheon and the spotless name.
" Why poor and lowly still ?"
                If thou wouldst know,
Their very virtues often keep them so.
The patient virtues of the labouring poor
Teach us to trust, to vanquish, or endure :
From them our *real* wealth and riches rise,
In them our nation's strength or weakness lies,
Not in the fools that would their worth despise.

(The strongest bough may not the loftiest be,
And sometimes we've to stoop before we see
The fairest peach we gather from the tree.)

Though the poor worker is our source of wealth,
He owns no riches but a stock of health—

A

The precious plank—the hope—the whole estate—
The all that parts him from a pauper's fate.
Though it may swamp, and must at last decay,
Cheerful he toils and trusts from day to day:
Across his sky so many clouds have pass'd,
He grows familiar with the threatening blast,
And trusts the future as he did the past.
The labouring poor!
     Faith's first-born sons are they;
The poor man's faith moves mountains every day.
With health declined, with want and woe oppress'd,
And all that tries by the severest test;
With bright'ning hope we've seen the poor expire,
Blessing the love that tried them in the fire:
This have we seen, and mark'd with holy awe
The peace that wrapp'd the pauper's bed of straw,—
Have seen, and learn'd with spirit lowly bent,
WHY the Glad Tidings
     First to them were sent.

One afternoon in Autumn,
    When the trees
Begin to yellow with the evening breeze,
A happy troop of rough-clad village boys
Made Melville woodlands echo with their noise;
Free and barefooted, here and there they sped,
Where'er the biggest boy or fancy led.
From spot to spot they hurry to and fro,
Now o'er the springy grass they wander slow,
Point to the spot where once a fox was seen,
And to the bushes where the nests have been;

.

CLARKSON GRAY.

—page 8.

Now watch the frisky squirrel with longing eyes,
And vainly try to clutch the tempting prize;
When, quick as thought, they see him perched on high,
And feel the satire twinkling in his eye.

Brambles and beech-nuts now their steps detain,
And now the varying pleasures change again :
They challenge, wager, boast, and disagree,
Then try who farthest up shall climb the tree ;
Then quickly leap with laughter to the ground,
And o'er the woodland path again they bound ;
Then, with a slacken'd pace, they slowly roam
Till the thought strikes them of returning home.
They mimic now the shrill steam-whistle's cry,
And off at railway speed
                    The urchins wildly fly.

But Clarkson Gray, a blooming bright-eyed boy,
Remain'd, another pleasure to enjoy,
For he had heard the pheasant's whirr of flight,
And stood to watch its beauty with delight.
A little ornithologist was he,—
Each little birdie was his portégé.
On sunny days, when cobbler Scott display'd
His gay canaries 'neath their cabbage-blade,
To watch the inmates of the prison bowers
He'd hang about the cobbler's door for hours.
He watch'd the pheasant long with wistful eyes,
And much admired its motion and its size,
When, like a prism on the spreading bough,
He mark'd its rainbow plumes with thoughtful brow.

Nothing on earth could with that bird compare,
The world, he thought, had nothing else so
        fair ;
Its sweeping form, its glorious, gleamy dyes,—
'Twas Nature's triumph in the boy's eyes.
Long he admired, and long he gazing stood,
His mates were gone, and silent was the wood ;
When, on the calm,
                He heard a feeble cry,
And, half afraid, felt half inclined to fly,
When louder still it pierced his startled ear,—
An infant, he felt sure, was wailing near.
With cautious step,
                With ear and eye attent,
Beneath the bending boughs he nimbly went.
When but a little farther in the wood,
Led by the piteous cry, transfix'd he stood,—
A horror seized the boy :
                His heart beat wild,—
'Twas old nurse Peggie and the Doctor's child :
Silent in death the faithful Peggie lay,
Where she had stay'd to rest,
                The child to play.
Instinctive terror urged the lad to fly,
Till duty heard again the piteous cry ;
Bravely he dash'd the terror from his heart,
And, stooping, quickly did the nobler part :
Gently he raised the infant from the grass,
Nor paused to soothe her infantine distress.
With rapid steps he left the dreary place,
And ten years older look'd his little face ;

Then doff'd his coat to shield her from the cold,
And wrapp'd her chilly limbs within its fold;
Then strove with all his boyish address
To still her cries, nor long without success,
And hush'd her aye with many a fond caress.
With cheering care he bore his tender load,
Soon left the wood and gain'd the public road.

The Doctor's house was just a mile away;
He hurried on, nor tarried by the way.
Lull'd by the motion of his rapid walk,
His song, his whistle, and his strange new talk,
The little bantling first grew quiet, then smiled,
And closer to his breast he held the child;
He kiss'd her little cheeks, her lips, her eyes,
He thought her like the babies in the skies,—
The little babies, spreading wings between,
Which in his mother's Bible he had seen.
Soon the road lessens as he trots away,
Conning the awful words he has to say:
Now he has reached the Doctor's little gate,
Where joy, grief, love, and gratitude await.

What grave results do seeming trifles yield!
In them what vast importance lies conceal'd:
Life, Death, and all that shapes our aims and ends,
On the mere dust of circumstance depends.
And Clarkson Gray, a toil-worn widow's son,
A new career of being has begun;
Stirr'd by the flutter of a pheasant's wing,
What strange new influences round him spring!

Next Monday morning found him bright with joy,
Dress'd in a fine new suit of corduroy;
With well-wash'd face, and hair comb'd smooth and neat,
And good new shoes and stockings on his feet;
His mother's heart with tender joy was full—
Her boy was enter'd at the Burgh School;
But burning blushes dyed the boy's face,
When at the lengthen'd bench he took his place.
The worthy Doctor kindly led him there,
And ere he left him stroked his sunny hair,
And whisper'd something of a father's care.

Now happy years in quick succession flew,
And Clarkson Gray in worth and stature grew;
Fond of his Latin, many a well-won prize
Brought floods of gladness to his mother's eyes,
On her old chest of drawers were they display'd,
And before visitors were proudly laid;
For, as she wiped them with her apron clean,
The pride she tried to hide by all was seen;
And as the liberal praise was duly paid,
She drank unquestion'd every word they said.
But Learning, day by day, with bright'ning rays,
Taught him the value of the *Doctor's* praise;
And loud his bosom beat when he would go
Up to the Doctor's house his prize to shew;
But, strange to say, it always beat the more
When little Jane would meet him at the door.

The more he learn'd, the more his books he loved,
And more and more the Doctor's love he proved.

But time speeds on—the happy school-time ends,
And now the laboratory he attends.
And a long time it takes him to survey
The wondrous things the Doctor's shelves display—
Strange creatures brought from many a foreign shore,
And things still stranger awed him more and more ;
But soon, when Nature's page he conn'd with care,
He read her hieroglyphics treasured there.

Pills and prescriptions now his thoughts engage,
He knows the proper dose for every age ;
Much useful learning in his brain he stores,
And o'er great books on chemistry he pores ;
Knowledge each day some principle expounds,
And things, thought simple once, are now found vast
    compounds.
Now cultured thought imparts to every face
A certain beauty that we love to trace,
And gave to Clarkson Gray's a most subduing grace ;
His bright eye beam'd with gratitude and truth,
And all said Clarkson was a handsome youth ;
But his chief ornament, that graced him more
Than beauty, science, or his Latin lore,
Was the deep love he to his mother bore.

One day his heart beat high with hope and joy,
When with a smile the Doctor said,—" My boy,
If I've bestow'd on thee some small regard,
Your good behaviour's been my great reward ;
But for the deed thou didst my orphan child,
In some degree I fain would be assoil'd,

But partial payment only can be made,—
Such debts can never to the full be paid.
You go to College, Clarkson, and I'm sure
Your application would success secure ;
But you have talent, and I have no fear
But yours will be a very bright career.
Till it is finish'd no expense I'll spare,
Then of my practice you shall have a share ;
And when I get too old you know, my boy,
Perhaps the whole of it you may enjoy."

Poor human nature !   O how blind are we !
Not into the next moment can we see.
The worthy Doctor ere a week went round
In bed one morn a placid corpse was found ;
Calm and serene had pass'd the fleeting breath,
He look'd as if he ne'er had tasted death.
Surprise and sorrow spread the district o'er :
Were they to see the good man's face no more ?
Could Dr Crawford REALLY BE NO MORE ?
The palsied pauper hears it with surprise,
And much he marvels as he weeping cries,—
"Strange one so good and useful should be ta'en,
And I a cumberer should so long remain !"
Then worldlings wondering ask—
                 "Has he died well ?"
But this the poor and needy best could tell,
Whose tears for him that day so thickly fell.

He dies not well, they say, who dieth poor,—
This is the worldling's maxim fix'd and sure ;

But there's *another* may his spirit twitch,—
He dieth ill indeed who dies too rich.

When the first sorrow falls upon the soul,
Passion rebels and will not bear control;
Though texts of Scripture faithful friends
    impart,
They strike the ear, but never reach the heart;
And poor Jane Crawford, new to earthly grief,
Knew not and sought not where to find relief.
Wildly she wept!
          Her heart's first stay was gone,
The only parent she had ever known.
Sorrow, like Him who touch'd with a live coal
The unclean lips, exalts the human soul,
Makes truth speak out in words of living fire,
Just indignation, or the soul's desire.
Clarkson that day with sorrow-stricken face
Held the fair orphan in a fond embrace:
" My love," he said, "for I have loved you long,
Lean on this faithful bosom and be strong,—
Strong in the strength that succours to the
    tomb,
And bears the spirit far beyond its gloom;
What my best friend design'd and hoped to see,
Leaning on God, I'll toil and strive to be.
I go!
      My love for thee is strong as death,
It would not perish with my parting breath;
Holy and sacred is my love for thee,
Holy and sacred be thy love for me."
  B

The Future !
       O what myriads are found
Threading the mazes of thy dreamy ground ;
Yon rosy urchin bounding through the fields,
That sight what joy to the father yields !
He wipes the sweat-drops from his bright'ning brow,
He hails the boy and leans upon his plough ;
And as with honest pride he loves to trace
The breadth of shoulder and the open face,
He builds some beauteous castle in the air,
And banquets at the feast that all may share ;
Thinks of the great ones who were peasant-born,
The glorious sunsets of the cloudy morn :
In the bright future,
            O what deeds are done,
What empires conquer'd, and what battles won !

Anticipation !
       How thy pictures glow
With living hope or frown with clouds of woe ;
Oft hast thou mail'd the human soul with might,
To rise triumphant to the gates of light,
And paralyzed and goaded with thy gloom
The gentle loving nature in its bloom,
And fill'd with modest worth, the suicidal tomb.

Behold the bright-eyed stag !
       His sprightly form
Clears every danger, bounds through every storm ;
A dauntless lustre lights his upward eye—
Like Hope, what creature is so loth to die !

A deathless daring heaves his panting breast,
Though at his heels destruction long hath press'd;
Bound for the covert of his faithful hind,
He breasts the flood, and leaves the hounds behind,
And gains the pasture of his native wild,
While every foe, by fearless hope, is foil'd.

Earth was a lifeless clod till it received
Its living soul, by the Creator breathed:
The silent Forces!
           Th' great living power,
That's moved the world since the inhaling hour.
Earth was chaotic till by Force inspired;
And mind achieves not till the soul has fired;
And oft a foretaste of some long'd for bless,
Has won fruition or secured success.

Ten years of honourable toil have pass'd,
And Clarkson Gray's achieved his end at last.
In chemist's shop he'd diligently served,
Shunning the froward, who from virtue swerved,
Attended classes, every chance improved,
And when at leisure dreamt of her he loved;
And when at eve he sought the Caltcn Hill,
What golden light would all his future fill!

Inspiring height!
           The great around thee now
Once roam'd the dreamland of thy classic brow.
On thee professor's chairs have first been won,
Ere the curriculum was well begun.

There painters first have heard the hum of praise,
And poets blush'd beneath the circling bays;
There Science, too, has cull'd her trophies fair;
And WORLD-WIDE VALOUR HAS BEEN CRADLED
    THERE!
Ah! noble youths have quaff'd thy spirit lore,
Whose bones now whiten on a foreign shore!

When Clarkson first wrote M.D. to his name,
Won by the toil of body and of brain,
Thoughts of the dead, who hoped to see that day,
Took part of his great happiness away.
A mother's patient toil, and deep-toned love,
           Time was not to repay:
Thus comes the chalice of long look'd for joy,
It never comes unmingled with alloy.

But now Jane leaves an aunt's protecting care,
The joys and toils of married life to share;
The sacred knot is tied without delay,
And now she smiles, the wife of Dr Gray.
A paltry sum is all their earthly store,
But, then! the coffers of their love run o'er;
And Hope says Fortune soon will make it more.
The happy pair now bravely settle down,
To try the practice of a country town.

Their little home, though riches might contemn,
Was quite a glorious paradise to them;
For precious gifts, and things exceeding fair,
More to be prized than rubies, nestled there.

Of knowledge both had gain'd a goodly store,
For both desired, and felt the need of more ;
And many trials had school'd their youthful heart,
Early to choose the sure and better part :
As use keeps metal from corroding rust,
Trials brighten faith, and fix the pious trust ;
And hearts that vibrate for the joys above,
Drink, even on earth, a deep, twice-sweeten'd love.
Now, though for years he toil'd with small
        success,
He loved his proud profession none the less ;
But, studying hard, pursued without a frown
The ill-paid practice of the country town.
And though no carriage dallied at his door,
'Twas well frequented by the labouring poor.
With kind concern he heard their various ills,
And much they prized his pity and his pills :
He knew his mission, and could well impart
The words of balsam to the drooping heart.
The modest *fee* he'd thankfully receive,
But oft, instead of getting, had to give.
Through years of toil, with little means to spare,
His darling science he pursued with care :
The borrow'd work, too dear for him to buy,
Is quickly scann'd, nor suffer'd long to lie ;
Important pages rapidly he jots,
And Jane at leisure takes the copious notes.
His threadbare coat he dons without regret,
But he must have his *Medical Gazette.*
For Science every sacrifice he'll make,
Loved for its own and human nature's sake.

His is the high-soul'd Simpson's* point of view,
And mercy the great END he ever keeps in view.
Ungenerous souls should ne'er physicians be :
Be sure his progress ends with his Degree
Whose soul's enamour'd of the golden fee.

Now Jane, though poor, was rationally proud,
And justly valued the unthinking crowd :
No dress was so becoming in her eye
As *just the one she could afford to buy.*
Her pride was *real*—not of the spurious kind—
Her heart was noble, and her soul refined ;
The feelings of the poor she'd blush to hurt,
But felt no shame to wash her husband's shirt.
His poorest patient she would kindly greet,
Nor shun the poorest creature on the street ;
Would not have shied Old Nannie with her milk,
For Folly wading in her web of silk.
The simple meal Jane's skilful fingers dress'd,
And though 'twas scant sometimes, 'twas fondly press'd.
Smiling, she'd say,—

         " 'Tis well that peace and health
Little depend on artificial wealth ;
For every end that's most to be desired,
'Tis wealth to know how little is required."

But though his practice brought him little bread,
To many a bright discovery it led ;
And the good Doctor, rich in light and love,
Had bread to eat that worldlings knew not of.

* The celebrated and humane Professor James Simpson of Edinburgh.

His various triumphs, though scarcely recognised,
By one, at least, were most devoutly prized ;
A rich reward was Jane's delighted face
When, bright with hope, he would minutely
    trace
His skilful treatment of the doubtful case.
How strong is pure, enlighten'd, hallow'd love !
Its firm foundations Fortune cannot move :
Ah ! Fortune needs more weapons than her own,
To quench the courage that's sustain'd *at home.*

True, there were times the faithless tear would
    start,
And faint misgivings would come o'er his heart,
For Jane's devoted love, and cheerful toil,
       Oft made his bosom smart ;
But, quick to mark the shadow in its fall,
With love's address, she'd his attention call
To some bright blessing in their humble lot,
Till all but love and duty was forgot.

Though poor and unsuccessful, well she knew
The Doctor's talent was surpass'd by few ;
And many a prayer on trembling Hope arose
That brighter prospects yet might interpose.
But when she saw him brook, with soul erect,
The look of coldness and the forced respect,
A spark of honest indignation burned,
And trembling Hope to strong conviction turned,
And in her soul the servile, purse-proud herd
       She loathed and spurn'd.

Prophetic Faith!

                Events were on the wing
That, more than e'er she dreamt of, were to
    bring.

At night,
How weird is Winter! when his locks of snow
Fall fast and thick on drifted heaps below!
The wrapp'd-up pilgrims glide along the streets
Like noiseless spectres in their winding-sheets;
Trees look unkindly at us through the dim—
We fear their ghastly figures, gaunt and grim:
But on the wild, strange feelings o'er us steal,
The awful voice of silence there we feel;
A death-like stillness gathers o'er and o'er,
And earth, so silent, looks like earth no more,
But, like some vast encampment of the dead;
Alone, the spirit-land we seem to tread,
           And, in an eerie dream,
We wonder if we too are with the dead!

One night in winter, at the midnight hour,
When earth's dark shadows o'er the spirit lower,
Yon lordly castle echo'd with the sound:
" Fly for the nearest doctor to be found!
Fly for the nearest! summon Dr Gray!
His Lordship's illness brooketh no delay!"
Nor was it long before the Doctor stood
Before his patient's couch in thoughtful mood.
Calm and collected, carefully he scann'd
The startling symtoms, and his treatment plann'd;

With keen perception was his judgment form'd,
The citadel of death at once he stormed ;
     No moment to be lost,
The urgent operation is, with calm dispatch,
     Most skilfully perform'd.

Now when the good Professor said next day,—
"My Lord! you owe your life to Dr Gray!"
His words were like the alchemy of old,
They changed the Doctor's prospects, stern and cold,
And made them bright with hope, and gleams of
    promised gold.
Now to the castle oft he took his way,
And now his practice better'd every day ;
And all had confidence to place in worthy Dr Gray.

Without position few can recognise
The light of genius, or its lustre prize ;
And e'en Columbus, while without a friend,
     All Europe could despise.
Without the glittering settings of success,
Men value diamond as they value glass ;
Pictures are judged of by their costly frames,
And books are valued for their author's names ;
And many now the Doctor patronise,
Who ne'er before his worth could recognise :
But "from the very first," *they say*,
     "They knew that he would rise."

Though years of practice have increased his fame,
And given a row of letters to his name,
  c

Ne'er have his labours for the poor decreased
But with his influence for good increased.

When in a mining village of his round,
Whole families crowded in one room he found,
He mourn'd that e'er such barb'rous dens should be
The frequent home of British industry;
And urged with zeal the worthy Squire to see
That labour's weal must wealth's best interest be.
" In one apartment !"
                         " Tell me," he would say,
" *Where* he who works all night may sleep all day ?"

In sickness, too, as everybody knows,
Life may depend upon an hour's repose;
I know what useful lives such dens have lost,
And you the widow's pensions they have cost.

A wise investment has it proved to be,
Those well-appointed houses that you see;
The one detach'd a little from the rows,
Is where the injured and the sick repose;
And there does Jane preside three days a week
To teach the art of cooking for the sick.

Now none could Jane's ingenuous face regard,
Nor see how much she felt her great reward;
Her Clarkson honour'd, prosp'rous, and esteem'd,
In every look the soul's oblation beamed,
And in her deeds of love a grateful language
      stream'd.

But now our muse to the Infirmary hies,
Where on a couch a weary patient lies;
He is discharged!
          This is the day,
The kind official says, he must away,—
Pronounced " Incurable."
             His doom he hears;
But, ah! it brings no Hezekiah's tears,
It is not Death the hopeless stranger fears.

Stunn'd for a moment with the mental pain,
That brings a kind of stupor o'er the brain,
An icy coldness at his heart he feels,
And o'er his frame a nervous tremor steals.
Yes, he must rise, must raise his feeble frame,
Must leave "the house," must face the world
    again;
Without a home, without a friend on earth,
The clerk alone can tell his place of birth.
His scanty clothing thin, and cold, and worn,
Hangs sad and loose upon his wasted form;
And many awkward stitches witness bear
To his unskilful efforts to repair.
Thin are his shoes, and their proportions say
They've been in other service in their day;
His long thin fingers o'er each other ply,—
White is his cheek, and glassy is his eye;
Spent by disease, convulsed and tempest torn,
Like the pale cloud that's drifted by the storm;
Slowly he reaches the Infirmary gate,
And, lingering, leaves it with a faltering gait;

The portress marks him with her practised eye,
And, sighing, bids the trembling wretch "Good bye."

What scenes of grandeur, harmony, and strife,
Are seen in the great Picture Gallery of Life ;
And in the bustle of the city street,
At every turn we breathing pictures meet.
The looks of gladness and the looks of woe
Leave on our soul their spectrum as we go.
Yon masculine dressmaker of Princes Street,
And now his starving seamstresses we meet ;
(The wealthy mercer, who'll subscriptions pay
To crush the sin he fosters every day !)
The pious lady, heartless as her sheaves
Of fabulous tracts that nobody believes ;
The true disciple, in God's service spent,
On some quiet deed of love and mercy bent.
The proud transgressor with untarnish'd name,
His victim skulking to the dens of shame ;
The pensive mother and the sickly child,
The happy school-boys with their gambols wild ;
The wretched youth in handcuffs led to jail,
And see yon invalid creeping like a snail.

The poor Incurable again we meet !
Slowly he seeks the unfrequented street ;
He gains the suburbs with a panting breast,
And, stopping, leans upon the wall to rest ;
A light barouche is slowly passing by,—
"Can it be meant for him ?
                    That kindly cry !"

" We're going south, young man ;
                        If that's your way,
You're welcome to a lift!"
                        Cried
                        Dr Gray.

Big tears now started to the stranger's eyes ;
He took his seat in silence
                        And surprise.
Jane, too, was there—a happy wife was she—
A darling boy was smiling on her knee.
She look'd with pity on the panting youth,
She felt his earnest, open gaze of truth ;
And on his pallid brow she mark'd the grace
That rudest fortune never can efface,—
The stamp of thought, that Fortune's wheel defies,
The look that rags conceal from vulgar eyes.

That night they spread the wanderer's couch of rest,
And charm a load of sorrow from his breast.
" Shall we," they say,
                        " So much from God receive,
Nor strive His hapless children to relieve ?
'Twere mockery then to say that we believe.
Unnumber'd are the blessings we possess,
Let deeds of love our gratitude express ;
We'll keep the homeless stranger till he dies :
There is no love where there's no SACRIFICE !"

Kindly they nurse him, as from day to day
We sadly pluck the wither'd leaves away

From some fair flower, whose blight we cannot
    stay.
From time to time his simple tale he tells;
But when fond memory o'er his mother dwells,
Then o'er his hollow cheek, with child-like sobs,
            The long pent sorrow wells.

Left unprotected at an early age,
Too soon in business did the youth engage;
Earnest and true, by generous thought
    inspired,
He lack'd the subtle tact that trade required,
And often left it for the calm retreat,
To sing of flowers that bloom'd among his feet;
With ruthless sweep the tide of ruin came,
And left him beggar'd, with a feeble frame.

With more than pity now, from day to day,
They mark the silent process of decay.
By many a soothing art relief they gave,
Smoothing the dreary passage to the grave.
Jane bent beside him at the evening prayer,
Then smooth'd his pillow with a mother's care,
And doubtless angels, though unseen,
           Were entertained there.

Now every woe has found the sweet surcease;—
Loving and leaning on the Prince of Peace,
Death finds him calmly waiting his release.
The weary heart shall palpitate no more,
The dream is ended, and the strife is o'er;

But on his breast they find, wrapp'd up with care,
A folded letter and—
                        A lock of hair :
The old, old story,
                        Love had builded there.
Again the treasure on his breast they place,
And *Christ-like* tears have fallen on his face.
And now, what's due to human dust the Doctor
        pays,
And in the grave, with deep, heart-felt respect,
                The stranger's head he lays.

For wandering dogs has Scotland raised a dome,
And has no shelter, but a pauper's home,
For her Incurables !
                        Whose feeble cry
Rebukes a nation's senseless luxury !
Well cared for dogs in thousands, wealth maintains
To hunt, where no wild thing, thank God,
        remains.
See ! horses, dogs, and men, 'mid horrid yells,
Hunting—far gentler creatures than themselves.
Surely, if hunting *really* were in view,
They'd go to India for a year or two !

O ye who e'en in health and strength repose
On cushion'd sofas, hear a brother's woes !
In yonder den,
                        Hear lingering disease
Beseeching Heaven for a moment's ease :

Tossing, he cries—
              " Would God that it were night !"
Then moans in anguish for " the morning light."
No yielding mattress there !
              His chaff and straw
Are hard and matted,
                      And,
              His joints are raw !
You cry, " Let him to the Infirmary go ;"
Alas ! on *it* too little ye bestow ;
They *cannot* keep the poor who die TOO SLOW.

O for a home where lingering Pain may rest,
And cureless wounds may to the end be dress'd !
'Twould profit Science,
              And, in mercy think,
'Twould mend some fibre of " *the broken link,*"
And make the bitter dregs of many a weary life
              Less ill to drink.
O Scotland, hear the weary, hopeless cry !
Say the bless'd ANODYNE you'll yet supply—
A place of rest, where poor Incurables may find relief,
              And in repose may die !

MISCELLANEOUS POEMS.

D

THE YEAR SIXTY-ONE.

I AM passing away!
I am passing away!
   Like the crowds that have gone before :
My smiles, troubles, and tears,
My sins, sorrows, and fears,
   And my follies will soon be o'er.

I am passing away!
I am passing away!
   And many a deed I have done :
Though I boast not of wars,
I am proud of my scars,
   And my fields neither fought nor won.

For I've lower'd the flag
Of a cheat and a brag—
   The greatest scamp under the sun ;
I have bow'd not to Mars,
But the stain'd Stripes and Stars
   Were rent up in old Sixty-one.

In a few fleet hours more
My brief life will be o'er :
   What is mere human power when done ?
Every life's but a part
Of the great human heart,
   That yet has to throb into one.

As my life ebbs apace,
Loving spirits retrace
   In sadness the deeds I have done ;
We'll not part as we met,
And they'll never forget
   The doings of old Sixty-one.

The old smiled at my birth
That lie cold in the earth ;
   But weary ones sleep not alone,
For the staff and the stay
I have hurried away,
   And the feeble left tott'ring on.

I have nipp'd from the stem,
Ay, life's loveliest gem,
   And I've wither'd the fairest bloom ;
I have gladden'd the heart,
And I've rent it apart,
   And buried bright hopes in the tomb.

There's a deep spirit power
In the still midnight hour ;
   And happy are they, I wot,
Who have never with fear
Seen the dark hour draw near,
   As they watch'd by the loved one's cot.

I have silver'd the hair
Of the maid bright and fair,
   I have whiten'd her cheek with woe ;
I have pierced bosoms keen
With wounds deep and unseen,
   The cold world never shall know.

But when memory breathes
Over hope's wither'd leaves,
   With sorrow the soul is o'ercast ;
For the leaf that is dry
Never stirs but to sigh
   For sunshine too lovely to last.

I have mated the old
With bright fetters of gold
   To the maid of sunny sixteen ;
I have scorch'd the old brain
With rancour and pain,
   Where visions of peace should have been.

I have bow'd down the head
In the battle for bread,
   And tried if the spirit were true,
And I've made it run o'er,
With a soul-saving ore,
   The lovers of gold never knew.

In the sink and the den
Of your lost fellow-men,
   I've heard the soul's shriek of despair ;
I have look'd with eyes moist
For the servants of Christ,
   But, how rarely I found them THERE !

In the palace of kings,
'Mid earth's costliest things,
   'Mid joys truth and virtue impart,
In that home of delight
I have heard in the night
   The deep wail of a widow's heart.

I am passing away !
But my spirit shall stay
   With many and many a one :
She'll look back through the years,
Dim with troubles and tears,
   And she'll live in old Sixty-one.

But the lives, if you'll trace,
Of our numerous race,
   In emotion you'll find we're one ;
The past ages impart
But a tale of the heart,
   And so will the ages to come.

Time will turn up the glass
When my last grain shall pass,
   And the sand shall be order'd anew,
It will not be changed,
But be newly arranged, —
   DISPOSAL alone shall be new.

Then prepare for the smiles,
Tears, troubles, and toils,
   And the duties that will not be few ;
Be faithful and strong
In repressing the wrong,
   And fearless the right to pursue !

THE MOOSIE.

MY certie, Moosie, ye're no blate—
  Ye loopie loon, ye's get your fee—
To stech yersel' wi' my bit laif,
  And crum'le a' the lave to me.

I doot, I doot, yer gusty gab
  Some dreadfu' death will gar ye dee;
I doot I'll hae to break the law
  O' sacred hospitalitie !

I dinna like the wily trap,
  Sae fu' o' a' black treacherie ;
But, then, ye mootle a' my bread,
  An' winna let my kebbuck be.

I'll hae to toast the wee bit cheese,
  And spread the scouther'd meal to thee,
Inveet ye to the Judas feast,
  An' gar ye drink yer ain dredgie.

But, Moosie, say that ye repent,
  An' I'll compound the thing wi' thee ;
A' orra bits s'all be yer ain,
  An' a' the moolins I s'all gie.

Though puss o' thee the hoose wad redd,
   I canna thole her fiendish glee;
Rejoicin', like the diel himsel',
   Owre some puir sinner's meeserie.

Sae, Moosie, be the real aefauld,
   An' nae sic death ye'll ever dee;
Ne'er mootle at my wheaten laif,
   An' let my wee bit kebbuck be.

Mind, I've to scart an' scrape mysel',
   I've pinglet sair for a' ye see;
Faith aften puts my kettle on,
   An' lippins for th' pickle tea.

———o———

ANNIE'S CROON.

I LOVE to see the sister seek
   A brother's guardian eye;
I love to see her lean upon
   His silent, safe reply.

I love to see the father's pride
   When his fair child is nigh;
I love to see the watchful love
   That lights the mother's eye.

E

She knows the laugh that mocks the heart,
   That drowns the struggling sigh ;·
She knows when there are tears to shed,
   Although the cheek be dry.

In sorrow's hour I love to see
   The soothing friend draw nigh ;
I know that friends have soothing words,
   For many once had I.

I love to see the maiden's cheek,
   When lover's steps draw nigh,
When rapture heaves her throbbing breast,
   And glitters in her eye.

I love to see her tingling cheek,
   Her hope-dilated eye ;
I know what rapture fills her heart--
   A lover too had I.

But changes came, and hardships press'd,
   And sorrows dimm'd my eye ;
Friends smiled, but not as they had smiled,
   And proud ones pass'd me by.

Aye, changes came, and Death bereaved,
   No mother then had I ;
And bitter tears in silence fell
   As years pass'd slowly by.

Tears are the truest things on earth,
  But oft in ambush lie,
When hopes are gone, and friends have flown,
  They gather in the eye.

I've toil'd with no unwilling hand
  Through many a weary day;
But while I ply my needle bright,
  My thoughts are far away.

I often dream old dreams again,
  Of girlhood's sunny skies,—
But, wake to find I've hoary hair,
  And glasses on my eyes.

———o———

GRATITUDE.

GIVE me, O Lord, a grateful heart,
  A thankful spirit give to me;
Whate'er Thou choosest to withhold,
  Withhold not gratitude from me.

When friendship breaks upon my path,
  And sheds its sunshine over me;
O may I, whilst I love the friend,
  The springs of action trace to Thee.

Upon the lofty Himalayas
  The sun pours down his burning sea;
But on their cold ungrateful brow
  Nothing but snows eternal be.

Thy blessings then, if not received
  As such, then such they ne'er shall be;
The atmosphere of gratitude
  Must bathe the rays that come from Thee.

The voyager of human life,
  Like him who ploughs the troubled sea,
Fears but the dangers overhead,
  And those that on life's surface be.

But terror would his soul appal,
  Could he the awful regions see
O'er which his tiny bark has pass'd
  Unscathed, because sustain'd by Thee.

When life is o'er, and perils past,
  And we life's woundrous chart shall see,
Songs of immortal gratitude
  Shall vibrate through eternity.

'Twere disrespect to God or man,
  To trust no further than we see;
The poorest wretch that begs his bread
  Resents THIS as an injury.

And Thou hast said, that living faith
  Should test each living soul's degree ;
The tribute we ourselves demand
  Dare we demur to render Thee ?

The hardest rock that ever frown'd
  Defiance to the land or sea,
Some fissure in its side we find,
  Where some sweet flower of beauty be.

The plan of Thy salvation, then,
  O let each darken'd spirit see,
That every living soul may glow
  With living gratitude to Thee ;

And where it is compassion dwells,
  For every child that strays from Thee ;
And hearts will burn, and hands will bleed,
  To bring the wanderer back to Thee.

Not pious words, not sounding praise,
  Not frequent bending of the knee,
Is gratitude ! 'tis *living* faith,
  Which through the creature serveth Thee.

Religion ! incense of the soul,
  No strange mysterious thing should be ;
'Tis spoken in a single word,—
  'Tis only gratitude to Thee.

Then, Lord, give me a grateful heart,
    A grateful spirit give to me ;
For, Lord, without a grateful heart,
    No living soul can worship Thee.

———o———

BONNIE MARY M'LEAN.*

WHAUR Neidpath Castle's hoary head
Hangs owre the bonnie winding Tweed,
Whaur mony a sough o' warlike deed
        Gangs wimplin' by,
An' glaiket lammies fearless feed,
        Nae danger by,—

There Mary smiled !   A fairer flower
Ne'er breathed owre brake, owre bank, or bower,
Her smile cam owre ye wi' a power
        She little kenn'd ;
Aye hearts broke for the bonnie flower,
        An' wadna mend.

Whaure'er her smouts o' feet had been,
The fairies vow'd by "a' thing green,"
That marks o' fairy feet were seen
        As clear as day ;
An', "Count the quorum !" cried the queen,
        "Some jaud's away."

* Granddaughter of Walter Laidaw of Chapelhope (scene of the
"Brownie of Bodsbec"), and maternal aunt of the author.

BONNIE MARY M'LEAN.

—page 88.

Her hair upon her breast did fa'
Like gowden licht on drifted snaw ;
An' fain wad Love stown some awa
      To kiss an' caimb,
An cuddle in his bosie-ba'
      Whan a' his lane.

Whan bathed in pity's pearlins bricht
Were her twa een o' mornin' licht,
Love's head grew dizzy at the sicht,
      Whan owre him fell
Their saft, subduin, hallow'd licht,
      Like heaven itsel'.

An' whan o' woman's love she sang,
The passin' spirits owre her hang,
For something owre the saul she brang
      That wasna grief—
But tears an' sighs, baith saft an' lang,
      Aye gied relief.

Tears stood whaur tears had never been,
For e'en *auld bachelors* were seen
To smuggle saut draps frae their een,
      An' hoastin' fa',
To smoor the sighs they sudna been
      Sae *dreich to draw*.

As wee white flower before it blaws
An inklin' o' its beauty shows,
Her teeth, the twa wee dazzling rows,
   Cam to the sicht,
White as the snawflake ere it fa's—
   Like streeks o' licht.

Her loesome lips sae red, sae rare,
Garr'd birdies flutter i' the air,
An' lang to licht on fruit sae fair;
   But, best o' a',
A word to wound a heart o' care,
   They ne'er loot fa'.

An' when she tried her love to speak,
The bashfu' roses fled her cheek;
Her tongue it wadna, wadna weet,—
   The bonnie doo;
The silent saul the love maun speak,
   Sae deep, sae true.

The hearts she made baith sad and sair,
Had aye to loe her mair and mair;
A flower wi' Mary's hallow'd air
   Ne'er bloom'd on Tweed,—
Sae guid, sae guileless, and sae fair,
   But,—Mary's dead!

THE EARLY FLOWERS.

THE early flowers! the early flowers!
  How welcome are the early flowers!
They come though still the tempest lowers;
  Who would not love the early flowers?

Their tender stems and timid bloom
  Sink not beneath the pelting rain;
But, crush'd by rude unheeding step,
  They perish, nor will rise again.

And not less fair the early flowers,
  That pledge our being's noblest goal;
Young aspirations, rudely crush'd,
  Breed many an ulcer in the soul;

And lost are Fortune's golden showers,
  And many a bright and noble fame;
Ah! many a spot bears bitter weeds,
  That might have waved with golden grain

With young emotion's beating breast
  Young fancy tries her infant powers,—
Wound not the fledgling's feeble wing,
  Crush not the spirit's early flowers.

F

Though sullied yet these flowers may be,
  Or choked on life's dry dusty road,
In sorrow's hour they wield a power,
  That leads the pilgrim's feet to God.

The early flowers! the early flowers!
  How lovely are the early flowers!
As leaflets dropt from angel-bowers,
  Let us revere the early flowers.

MY BLANKET SHAWL.

Aul' frien', ance mair come frae the kist,
  For ye are ane that ne'er grew caul';
Ye dichtit aye the hidden tear,
  Thou wae, thou weel-worn Blanket Shawl.

O! wae is me, that dreadfu' nicht,
  My lammie's feetie grew sae caul';
Within thy faulds she breathed her last,—
  Thou sad, thou sacred Blanket Shawl.

An' whan I gaed to sell my tapes,
  To screen the rest frae want an' caul',
I fear'd the sicht o' faces kent,
  An' owre me drew my Blanket Shawl.

Whan queans wad answer to my rap,
  Wi' uppish gait an' voices bawl;
I turn'd awa' maist like to drap,
  An' tichter drew my Blanket Shawl.

Ungratefu' body that I was,
  I sudna been sae stung withal;
I sud hae fix'd my thochts on Him,
  Wha aye saw through my Blanket Shawl.

But better fortune smiled on me,
  My laddies noo are stout an' tall;
But aye I hear a manly sigh
  Whan oot I tak my Blanket Shawl.

———o———

MY MITHER TONGUE;

A SOUGH FRAE THE FAR LAND.

My mither tongue's a kindly tongue,
  An' fu' o' sympathie;
O it hath breathed the kindest words
  That e'er were breathed to me.

The words that winna leave the heart,
  Whate'er its anguish be;
That lie within its livin' tide,
  Like pearls in the sea.

The tongue I hear's nae kindly tongue,
　　It soun's sae cauld an' hie,
It rudely smites the weary heart,
　　An' canna comfort gie.

The weary heart is like the bird
　　That's chased frae tree to tree,
An' unco fain wad be at rest,
　　But kens nae whaur to flee.

Though loudly sings the briny wave,
　　An' bricht its waters be,
The weary wanderer canna drink
　　The waters o' the sea.

But O the tongue that first I heard
　　Upon my mither's knee,
Can aye gie solace to the heart
　　Nae ither tongue can gie.

My mither tongue! my mither tongue!
　　Sae fu' o' sympathie;
I fain wad hear my mither tongue
　　Ance mair before I dee.

THE DEAD CANARY.

My birdie's deid! my birdie's deid!
My bonnie birdie, thou art deid!
I've lost a fau'tless frien' indeed,
      Baith kind and true;
An' music's lost as sweet a reed
      As e'er she blew.

Nae mair I'll pu' the chicken-weed,
Nae mair I'll pu' the grun'sel heid,
Nor wander whaur wi' temptin' seed
      The rat-tail springs;
Nae mair for them ye'll cock yer heid
      An' flaff yer wings.

Whane'er ye heard my fit come in,
Yer chirp o' welcome wad begin,
Alang yer stickie ye wad rin
      To tak my ee,
An' deave me wi' yer kindly din
      To speak to thee.

Then ye wad set yer wee bit heid
An' "cheep" for sugar'd bits o' bread,
But try to dab my thooms instead ;
　　　　An' through yer cage
Wad crousely stap yer tappit heid
　　　　In mimic rage.

Syne ye wad mak yer neckie sma'
Whane'er I turn'd to gang awa,
An' cheep regret whan to the wa'
　　　　I hung ye up :
A bitter drap, noo ye're awa,
　　　　'S fa'n in my cup.

O mony a change has come an' gane
Sin' little Willie brocht ye hame,
An' boasted aye ye were his ain
　　　　Wi' pridefu' glee ;
As frae the paper-pock sae fain
　　　　He set ye free.

Hoo blythe we ran an' brocht ye meat,
An' watch'd to see hoo ye wad eat,
An' jumpit whan sae loud an' sweet
　　　　We heard ye sing ;
An' leugh whan ye yer neck wad streek
　　　　An' spread yer wing.

They're gane wha linger'd whaur ye hang,
They're gane wha' kept the ingle thrang,
Whan sunny hope made glad the sang
    An' bricht the ee ;
Whase faithfu' spirits aften lang
    To dicht my ee.

Ah ! whiles I thocht ye wae to see
The tears I hid frae a' but thee,
For ye a waesome note wad gie,
    Sae saft an' lang ;
An' something mair than melodie
    Wad swell thy sang.

Wha kens what griefs hae whiles distress'd,
Thy wee bit breastie noo at rest ;
Some hidden spunk within thy breast
    Has maybe burn'd ;
Some nestlin' dearer than the rest
    Ye've maybe mourn'd.

But then, when sorrow droop'd thy wing,
Ye cud yer sorrows sweetly sing,
An' wafted far ye'd seem to hing
    Upon yer lays,
Till rapture wi' its fiery wing
    Consumed thy waes.

An' sorrows aften cease to be,
When we frae earth but rise awee ;
For brichter laurels tak the ee
      Than earth e'er grew,
Or fancy's flowery fingers gie
      The burnin' broo.

What garr'd thee struggle to resign
The spatless, blameless life o' thine ?
O is there for thy vocal kin'
      Some ither sphere ?
Fareweel ! O thee I'm laith to tine,
      But daurna speer.

Whan ye began to droop yer wing,
An' chirle what ye cudna sing,
The trim'lin' tear it used to bring.
      Noo sair I greet ;
An' lang will I for thee, sweet thing,
      My winkers weet.

My loof has been yer deein' bed,
Ae faithfu heart for thee has bled ;
But, birdie, there are nane to shed
      A tear for me ;
Nae han' by sweet affection led
      Shall steek my ee.

LOVE.

It dawn'd on me first
Like a dreamy thing,
   Like a vision of fleecy white ;
In silence it came
And enveloped my soul
   In the folds of its mystic light.

A shadow had lain
Like a cloud o'er my soul ;
   My heart was a joyless thing ;
It came, and I felt
Like one that is waked
   By the touch of an angel's wing.

It came to my soul
Like the smiles of heaven
   When they fall on some lonely stream,
And gladden its breast
Till another heaven
   Its radiant waters seem.

G

It came like the spirit
Of infant morn,
   With her harp of ten thousand strings,
Yet stealing and soft
As a mother's voice,
   When she whispers of holy things.

O it pour'd a balm
O'er my troubled heart,
   That thrill'd to its inmost core—
I felt that I loved
With love that would last,
   Aye, when time was to me no more.

For it swept the cords
Of a deeper joy
   Than comes to perfection here ;
The cords of a love
That weddeth the soul
   To a brighter and holier sphere.

Then, O full of joy
Will the accents be,
   That shall pass with my parting breath ;
For the ties of the soul
But tighten the more
   When touch'd by the finger of Death.

MY WAG-AT-THE-WÂ'.

MY WAG-AT-THE-WA'.

Psalm xxxi. 24; Matthew x. 29, 30, 31.

My Wag-at-the-wa' is a bonny wee clock,
Fu' crouse and fu' kindly comes ilka bit stroke ;
It cheer'd up my heart when my hopes were but sma'
The "tick" o' my cantie wee Wag-at-the-wa'.

They crack o' their aight-day anes bein' sae true,
Their soun's like the soun' o' the wae cushie doo,
Ilk eeriesome stroke, like a "*warnin'*" does fa',
But blythe is the tick o' my Wag-at-the-wa'.

Langsyne when my dainty "*providin'*" cam hame,
I buskit wi' pride the bit house o' my ain,
An' never was hoosie mair couthie an' braw,
An' bricht was the face o' my Wag-at-the-wa'.

Wi' him that garr'd a' look sae bonny and fair,
The years slippit by without sorrow or care,
As king o' a' wonders our wee bairnies saw
The wonderfu' warks o' the Wag-at-the-wa'.

But death still'd the heart that aye loed me sae weel,
And deep was the sorrow my bosom did feel ;
Whan tears frae my faitherless lammies did fa',
I thocht that my heart wad hae burstit in twa.

Then dark grew the warl' that ance was sae fair,
My pouch sune grew licht, an' my housie grew bare;
I grat ower my bairnies sae helpless and sma',
An thocht I wad pairt wi' my Wag-at-the-wa'.

But a frien' startit up whaur least I had hope,
An' O we ne'er wanted the bite an' the soup;
I thankfully toil'd, tho' my earnin' was sma',
An' aye my bit clockie gaed waggin' awa.

Whan harvest cam roun' I aye shore for my rent,
An' aye to the schule my wee bodies I sent;
They tuk to their "lair," an' were likit by a',
An' noo keep their mither fu' bien an' fu' braw.

O mony bit struggle I've haen i' my day,
An' whiles I've been weary when steep was the brae;
But the very wee birdies unkenn'd canna fa',
An' the strength was aye gi'en me to warstle awa.

Nae doot whan my clockie an' me are our lane,
We've mony bit crack o' the days that are gane;
My heart turns grit, an' the tears thickly fa',
Whan saft grows the sough o' my Wag-at-the-wa'.

THE EVERGREEN;

OR,

THE MOTHER'S MEMORY.

Put in the drawer,—my heart can bear nae mair,- –
Row up the paper wi' my lassie's hair,
I ken !—I ken !—it but renews my waes,—
I ken I sudna touch my dautie's claes ;
But when the past comes croudin' through my brain,
I canna let her bits o' things alane.
The very bits o' clouts she daiker'd wi'
Are unco dear and precious things to me ;
Ah ! no a thing o' her's but has the power
To nip my breast an' gar my heart rin owre.

Nae mair frae 'hint the door I'll see her keek,
Nae mair to mine she'll lay her dimpled cheek ;
Ah ! never mair me roun' the neck she'll tak,
Nor douk her bonnie headie in my lap.

I dream'd a dream afore she took her bed,
An', oh ! waes me ! it's been owre truly read ;
An' frae the cock began to craw at nicht,*
I bodit aye that something wasna richt ;
An' ance the window shook frae head to fit ;
An' garr'd my very heart loup aff the bit.

* Superstitions common in the humbler walks of Scottish life.

Weel she was loed by ilka neebor wean,
An' unco blythe she keepit my hearth-stane ;
Whan ane wad greet she'd pleaser't sae aul' farran,
Wad let it see " the man that broke the barn,"
Wad mak doos' dookits wi' her fingers sma',
An' raise a lauch that wad divert them a' ;
Syne let them see upon the auld kist head
Hoo " Robbie Salmon "† selt his gingerbread ;
Wad cock her head an' gie sic pawkie looks,
Her tonguie gaun as it wad clippit clouts.

But, whan my wee drap tea I set a gaun,
My wee bit lassie sune was at my haun' ;
A drappie i' the saucer aye she gat,
An' syne contentit at my fit she sat—
But noo !
       When I sit doon,
              I scarce break bread,
I scarce can lift the saucer to my head ;
Ah ! never mair at nippit cakes I'll gowl,
Nor catch her fingers i' the sugar bowl.
Sin' e're she dee'd
           I wauken wi' a start,
An' somethin' awfu' sair comes owre my heart ;
The truth like lichtnin' min's me o' her death,
An' for a while I canna draw my breath ;
But when I dream, an' dawt her broo sae white,
I maistly wauken wi' the blest delight ;

† A Confectioner in Kirkcaldy, whose attendance at "Fairs"
rendered him a great favourite with the young.

I drink the joys that evermair hae ceased—
Tichtly I haud her to my heavin' breast;
For something strikes my heart as cauld as airn,
The terror—that again I'll lose my bairn;
I wauken wi' the dread o' what's ower true,
An' draps o' sweat are stan'in' on my broo.
I've grown so donnert, when I've laid things by,
I canna mind or think o' whaur they lie.
A hunder times I let my wark alane,
But thocht aye drives me to the wark again;
I canna read, for aye my grief breaks out,
An' maks me glad to rise an' gang aboot.
I ken!—I ken!—she's in a warl' noo,
Amang the flowers that Death can never pu';
I ken! oh! *weel* I ken we're born to pairt,
But,

      Woman!

               If I didna greet—

                             I'd break my heart!

I'VE MET THE LOOK.

I'VE met the look that makes the tear,
  The dazzling tear of rapture start,
To bathe the balmy buds of bless,
  From grateful pulses of the heart.

I've met the look that withers hope,
  And makes the tingling cheek grow pale;
The look that speaks the hollow heart,
  Without the cold and bitter tale.

I've met the look that darkens life,
  And blights the nurslings of the soul,
That makes the heart a dreary spot,
  And yet forbids the tear to roll.

Bear yet a while, thou throbbing heart,
  Thy weary strife will soon be o'er;
The wildest wave that swells the sea,
  Must soon expire upon the shore.

Bear yet a while, thou throbbing heart,
  You'll soon be still within my breast;
The wildest blast must *yet* be still,
  Must murmur low and sink to rest.

RETRIBUTION.

PART I.

THE WEE LADDIE'S PRAYER.

Scene—Public-House.

O COME awa hame, faither,—come awa hame !
My mither's aye vex'd when ye dinna come hame ;
She's no very weel, an' she's sittin' her lane,
O come awa hame, faither,—come awa hame !

O come, for ye ken a' the shops 'll steek in,
The sark's to be wash'd, and there's things to get in ;
I'll tak hame this bit bread, for my mither has nane,—
O come awa hame, faither,—come awa hame !

The nicht, when I gaed for some meal to my mither,
They tell'd me to gang awa back for the siller ;
My mither was vex'd, but I bade her no care ;
But her cheek's awfu' white, and her head's awfu' sair.

Dinna send me awa ! let me gang wi' yersel,
My mither's aye fear'd sin' the nicht that ye fell ;
An' *"the wife"* bade me "no trail here through the weet,
An' mark a' her hoose wi' my dirty bare feet."

O rise and come wi' me,—I'll lead ye my lane !
The neebours compleen, min', o' whan ye come hame ;
An' though they ken fine that my mither's no weel,
They've craved us the nicht for the bowlfu' o' meal.

H

I'll licht ye the pipe, if ye want a bit draw ;
Noo! stap doon the dottle, and syne come awa ;
For fear it gangs out, here's anither bit licht,—
But—faither—ye'll no strike my mither the nicht ?

Ae! she's vex'd whan she thinks that the neebours 'll tell,
But greets just, an' says that ye wisna yersel ;
I ken fine she greets, though, whane'er she's her lane,—
O come awa hame, faither,—come awa hame !

PART II.

O wae's me for sin *whan its found in distress !*
It gets mony a kick when it hasna address ;
But on this side the grave it has little to fear,
As lang as it hauds a guid grip o' the gear.

There's a doit'd auld body that trails through the street,
In the dourest o' days the auld body ye'll meet ;
Cauld, waesome, and weary, he trails through the toon,
Through the wind an' the weet, till he's like to fa' doon.

When he gaed to " the Boord" for a mite i' the week,
They drave him clean stupid, nae word cud he speak ;
Though their hearts cudna feel, they cud a' loodly storm
At the sins they themsels wad do weel to reform.

Nae heart yearns noo for the soun' o' his fit,
For him never mair will the late watcher sit ;
Although there's a Throne a' maun beg at ere lang,
Nane forgie him like Jeanie, wha suffer'd the wrang.

He hoasts an' he hankers, an' hings by his lane,
A' hearts noo to him are as hard as the stane ;
He gets ilka bite wi' the bark and the blame,—
Nae wee laddie noo coaxes him awa hame.

Daized, doit'd, and dirty, he trails through the toon,
At naebody's fire daur the body sit doon ;
Heart-hunger'd and cauld, whan he eats his bit bread,
His een are like stanes as they stare frae his head.

The puir body's followed by a' the wild weans,
They pelt him wi' dirt, an' they pelt him wi' stanes ;
An' Christians gang by, while at this they are thrang,
Wi' pomp an' wi' pride, as if naething were wrang.

He's a wae sicht to see whan the nicht-schule comes out,
Hoo he growls whan the wild laddies gather aboot ;
They "Hee!" and "Hurrah!" him, as roon' him they stan',
An' wild grows the looks o' the feckless auld man.

They knock aff his hat, an' they pu' his coat-tails,
Like a laddie he rins, like a laddie he rails ;
To get him to fa' a' the young heathens plan—
Ye wad greet at the sicht o' the sprawling auld man.

His face noo's as white as the hair o' his head,
An' O ye wad wish that the body were dead!
But he creeps to his feet, although nane len' a han',
An' short comes the breath o' the weary auld man.

To the outstan'in' cart noo he warstles awa,
An' he groans as he hurstles aneath the lock straw;
But the cart's to be yokit whan glimmers the dawn,
An' roughly they'll wauken the weary auld man.

Cauld nicht brings him back wi' as weary a heart,
But the nicht his auld een canna licht on the cart;
He hings at the place whaur the cart used to stan',
But there's nae bed the nicht for the weary auld man.

Ae frien' winna flee him, the last and the best,
Tho' cauld is her bosom, O still is her rest;
She wauks nae the weary whan glimmers the dawn,
Sae her lap is the lair o' the weary auld man.

There's a wild weary wail as he lays himsel doon,
There's the soul-stricken cry that nae tempest can **droon**;
"O Saviour o' sinners hae mercy on me!"
Is heard by the angels o' mercy on hie.

At first there's the dark panorama of life,
With the weapons of war that were lost in the strife;
There's the deep tide of woe, there's the anguish and pain,
There's a Spirit says—"Weary one, come awa hame!"

It's a dream on the earth, but it's nane in the sky,
For Jeanie is pleadin' wi' Guidness on high;
She aye points to the sorrow an' lichtlies her wrang,
And Love lets her gae for the weary auld man.

PART III.

Like a wee wauk'ning wean wi' a half-open ee,
Mornin' keeks owre the hill frae aneath her ee bree;
The cuddlin' wee cluds like the fleece roon' her fa',
Like the kind cozie claes o' a wee beddie-ba'.

The wee birdies wauken, their welcome to gie,
Syne "chirrip" an' fyke wi' their feathers awee;
An' some wayfarin' bodies look waesome an' lang
At the sair-worn clay o' an' auld beggar man.

There's a smile on the lip, tho' the lid's owre the ee,
There's a look ye wad thocht that nane like him could gie;
It's the look that was gien to the spirit that brang
The lang, lang'd-for release o' the weary auld man.

A cart passin' by taks him into the toon,
An' in the auld toon-house the sleeper's laid doon;
They send aff in haste for the auld parish wricht,
For they want the auld banes to be buried the nicht.

There's a deep living lore ilka wayfarer meets—
The wisdom that utters her voice in the streets;
While she whispers "Beware!" love and mercy we learn,
For the waif and the outcast was somebody's bairn ;—

Was ance a bit wean no the hicht o' yer knee,
An' pure as the spirits that wait us on hie ;
But whan wounded by thieves, and whan sorrows betide,
Priest and Levite whiles pass on the opposite side.

The weel-tended floorie that blooms i' the sun,
Wad dee on the wild whaur the weeds overrun ;
An' the weak an' neglected 'tis duty to grieve,
For they canna weel render wha dinna receive.

Oh, *the wicked are only the weak ones o' earth,*
The mourn'd o' the Saviour—the cause o' His birth ;
Tho' the wise and the prudent have sinn'd not as they,
They have sinn'd in their pride, or in *some other way.*

Tho' nane greet for him, tho' nane sich owre his lair,
Tho' nane slips awa wi' a lock o' his hair,
Holy tears o' affection for him hae been shed,
And a fond mother hung owre his wee cradle bed.

But owre his auld breast there is something row'd up,
It's heavy an' hard, they maun hae't rippit up ;
"It's siller ! it's siller, faith !" ilka ane says,
An' they greedily glaum at the auld body's claes.

They rive doon the rags o' his auld duds to see,
But they rive them in vain, for nae siller had he;
It's only the buttons an' bool that were ta'en
Frae the wee jacket pooch o' the laddie that's gane.

There's a growl, an' a curse, an' a fearsome gaffaw,
As they fling the wee bool and the buttons awa;
"He's been daft, the auld sinner!" cry a' in the place,
An' their gruesome looks glour owre the calm sleepin' face.

They hurry the job noo as fast as they can,
An' roughly they handle the sleepin' auld man;
The joke an' the jibe mingle up wi' the soun'
The pauper's wricht maks when he's nailin' him doon.

The auld bellman comes noo to tak out the dead,
An' wags to the tykes that tak up the close head;
Nane tell them to wait, an' the four lend a han',
An' aff gaes the last o' the weary auld man.

Nane join wi' the four as they gang doon the street—
But—the time-serving servant of Jesus they meet;
To a prosperous villain he touches his hat,
And—gangs by them caressing his dainty cravat.

A hoary-hair'd mortal creeps out to the licht,
An' mutters in wrath as he watches the sicht,
"If a lord's mickle dog to be buried were gaun,
They wad gang wi' the dog—aye, a hunder for one,—
That wad gang to the grave wi' an auld beggar man!"

WE A' HAE A SOMETHING.

"What thou knowest not now, thou shalt know hereafter."

WE a' hae a something, be't grit or be't sma,
To rich an' to puir there's a something to a';
Yer gear may be rife, or yer gear may be scant,
Ye'll aye hae a something ye'll think ye cud want.

It's whiles a bit thing o' mair bather than grief,
Like a jag i' the thoom, or a seed i' the teeth;
An' whiles it's a something o' sorrow an' care,
That wearies the spirit an' whitens the hair.

But, though ye be weary, though sair and unseen,
The saut silent tears fa' like pease frae yer een;
Be still! an' frae virtue an' faith dinna swerve,
For yer sorrow has some hidden purpose to serve.

For just as the insect, wha's sting is sae sair,
Consumes a' thing deadly that poisons the air;
The sorrow ye suffer, though deep be its scar,
Has saved ye frae something a thousand times waur.

Then dinna be faithless! for, oh, if ye trust,
Yer heart will be glad tho' ye dine on a crust—
The wealth o' the wilderness little we prize,
Whan the heart has a hame far awa i' the skies.

An' sorrow brings sympathy under its wings,
For sorrow aye saf'ens the heart that it wrings;
O let my tears fa', though they fa' like the rain,
On the breast that has bled wi' a grief o' its ain.

Our thochts an' our feelings it serves to refine,
An' gies them a touch o' the bricht an' sublime;
For spirit ne'er springs to the place o' its birth
Till stung by the sorrows that sadden the earth.

The cauld-hearted warl' aye meets wi' a smile,
For tho' yer heart's breakin' an' bleedin' the while,
When cometh the tempest, when strong is the tide,
Ye s'all find there's an Angel o' Strength by yer side.

Then bear wi' yer something, whatever it be,
Wi' the courage that Heaven's aye waitin' to gie;
An' think o' His words to the children o' men,—
What ye dinna ken here, ye hereafter s'all ken.

I

SPRING.

SEASON of promise ! and of gladness come,
In all thy former sweetness come again,
Break in on Winter's dark and gloomy reign,
And bless Creation with thy annual smiles.

Welcome the tints of thy returning glow,
Whose progress calls to mind a future hope,
And cheers the falling victim of despair,
To taste the pleasures of ethereal bliss.
With seeming joy the fertile kingdom smiles,
In glorious answer to the welcome call ;
And, with refulgent beauties to reveal,
Unfolds its bosom to the azure sky.
No more the chilling blasts of northern climes
Sweep through the forest with relentless rage ;
But soft showers fall, and gentle breezes blow,
In sweet obedience to thy softening sway.

Though Winter threatens oft to seize thy power,
And snatch the sceptre from thy gentle hand,
Yet wrath and love can never long contend ;
And as the tender smiling child of weeks,
That holds its treasure with tenacious grasp,
"Cooing" and smiling at the strong man's strength,
That seems arrested by some mystic power,
So reignest thou, O sweet subduing Spring !

And
      Though he scowls upon thy growing charms,
And fain would blight the buds that deck thy brow,
Thy smiles illume his clouds of coming storm,
Till they seem faithless to his angry power;
Then from thy cheering presence he retires,
Howling impatience at thy reign of love.
He is the despot of the snowy world,
And like all despots he is fain to blast
All that can bless and beautify the world;
Growth is arrested by his iron touch,
And all that's beauteous withers in his grasp!
      Sweet Liberty must die, or it must *sleep*,
And only dream of Freedom's sunny skies;
The meanest streamlet is afraid to sing,
For Freedom is the spirit of its song.

The mighty Sea! so turbulent and proud,
That roars defiance to all else beside,
Is by the tyrant shackled like a slave;
Nought can resist him but the light of Heaven,
The glorious spirit of inspiring Spring!

But O hath Winter not a counterpart?
Is his not like the cruel despot's reign,
The icy chain and the unsparing blast,
Bearing destruction to the fairest flower
That dares to lift a hopeful eye to heaven,—
Blighting its beauties till they sweep the earth?
Dark Winter's creatures these!—are they not like
The ruthless Haynaus of the human race?

But there's a spring of everlasting truth !
O come thou blessed day-spring from on high,
Cheer the fallen victim of the despot's wrath,
And chase away the Winter of the Soul !

———o———

FLOWERS.

FLOWERS are the heart's first offering.
   When first the wond'rous Flowers we see,
With dancing eyes we clutch the prize,
   And bear them to our mother's knee.

The weary wanderer's tatter'd child
   Sits dreaming o'er them with delight,
And while he dreams, their beauty seems
   To touch his infant soul with light.

And oft their balmy breath shall bless
   The vagrant's nightly-purchased lair,
And—half asleep—he'll strive to keep
   The blooms that Fancy gather'd there.

The Flowers no base-born homage pay,
   They court not wealth, nor power, nor state ;
They wear one bloom, breathe one perfume,
   At pauper's door and palace gate.

They shrink not from the poor man's touch,
   Nor from his old coat's rusty hue;
Despite the patch—*almost* a match—
   And darn that slyly jilts the view.

The tea-pot at old Nannie's pane,
   Though maim'd and marr'd with crack and craze,
Regales her sight with blooms as bright
   As ever glow'd in marble vase.

The proud, the paltry, hollow herd,
   Who ne'er saw worth where wealth was not,
Might (could they feel) here something steal
   Like censure, from old Nannie's pot.

But "earthy" they, and "of the earth,"
   They prize not man, but MAN'S ESTATE;
Mere "bread alone" they live upon,
   And dance mere *flunkies* to the great.

THE STORM.—A FRAGMENT.

I AWAKE in the woods with a struggling sigh,
And the quivering leaves whisper I am nigh;
Then the timid flowers in wood and lea
Bend low as they hide their sweets from me.
I breathe! and the winding mountain brook
In silence dims at my threat'ning look,

Then wanders forth with a hollow voice,
And the listening banks no more rejoice ;
For its murmurs low have a sadd'ning hum
Of the struggling waters yet to come.
Darkly I frown from the black'ning sky,
And the lightnings dart from my angry eye ;
I utter my voice !
           And the clifty rock
Tells me he "heeds not the voice that spoke."

OUR RAINY DAYS.

Dreep, dreep, dreep,
  Dreepin' ilka day ;
Rise ye bricht and bonnie sun,
  And chase the cluds away.
The weary weans, they winna please,
  They skirl a' the day ;
The bits o' creatures canna get
  Out owre the door to play.
If slicht-o'-han' John Frost were here,
  He very sune wad shaw,
Hoo he can change the jaws o' rain
  To bonny ba's o' snaw.

Dreep, dreep, dreep,
  Dreepin' ilka day ;
Rise ye bricht and bonnie sun,
  An' chase the cluds away ;—
Keekin' sleely out aneath
  Yer haps o' leaden grey,—
Creepin' out o' sicht again,
  And winna rise the day.
Rise up frae yer gowden bed,
  Fling yer haps away,
An' let us see what bonny sheets
  O' siller licht ye hae.
Look out owre the dreary cluds,
  An' tell them a' to gae ;
Or smile upon them, bonnie sun,
  An' kiss them a' away.

Dreep, dreep, dreep,
  Doon the plashes fa' ;
In comes little Johnica,
  Droukit like a craw.

THE HIGHLY RESPECTABLE MAN.

ISAIAH lviii 5, 6, 7; MATTHEW xxv. 31, to the end.

IT is long since "the world" he learned to despise,
It is long since its riches were dung in his eyes;
And yet, strange! in its wisdom no dodger can plan
Half so well as the "Highly Respectable Man."

'Tis but "humanly speaking" his wealth is his own,
For he piously looks on't as merely a loan;
And although he got all by a nice little plan,
He's really a "Highly Respectable Man."

When the poor are insulted, traduced,* or oppress'd,
No upright indignation by him is express'd;
It is most "injudicious" such matters to scan,
And becomes not the "Highly Respectable Man."

* Gold being a perfect metal, is highly tenacious, and consequently capable of great expansion; but there is a base one which far exceeds it in this respect; its name is *Calumny*,—a little of it goes a great way.

But when it goes so far as to cause wealth and affluence to withhold their charity from a poor defenceless orphan, whom consumption had rendered a pauper, we are reminded that names do not change substances, and that the name of Christian does not constitute one.

The "Old Burgh," for which this note is intended, will remember, in the case of the poor Factory Girl, in what manner they treated the *injured* and the *injurer*. Yea, with what Pharisaical indifference they saw the innocent abused, and the Father of the fatherless insulted.

But he knows that a Christian's duty is *this :*
A most rigid ATTENDANCE TO HEAR WHAT IT IS ;
And so absent from church let them catch him who can,
For he's *really* a " Highly Respectable Man."

Though misfortune's a crime, 'tis his duty to blame,
Though the naked and hungry entreat him in vain ;
He will talk of " Revivals " and each mission plan,
For he's *really* a " Highly Respectable Man."

Though the wretched around him his joys cannot mar,
He will rave of the heathen of Old Calabar ;
Of how many were "struck" when "the work" first began,
For he's really a *" serious,"* excellent man.

Though his eye never dimm'd, though his heart never
    bled,
For the " waif" that the honour'd and proud have
    misled,
He will talk of his " views," of his creed, and its plan,
For he's really a *pious*, " Respectable Man."

But the canting, self-righteous, compassionless crew,
Were the spirits the Saviour of men never knew ;
And the cup of cold water that mercy bestows,
Bringeth joy that the pitiless soul never knows.

The wealthy seducer, too's, cloth'd with respect,
And his crimes e'en the Churches will fail to detect ;
It is only UNFORTUNATE SINNERS they ban,
For they never affront a " Respectable Man."
    J

All his thoughts and opinions are studied with care,
For he's prize No. 1 'mong the *pure* and the fair;
And the prudent mamma will do all that she can,
To make sure of the " Highly Respectable Man."

There's a law for the weak, and a law for the strong,
There is wrath upon wrath for the VICTIM of wrong;
For the Bible is woman's, her sins to condemn,
But "SOCIETY's voice" is the standard of men.

Ah! 'tis only the BLUNDERING rogue men despise,
But the consummate villain's a "prince" in their eyes;
While with cool daring tact he can brave out his plan,
He's a "great," he's a highly "Respectable Man."

HONOUR, VIRTUE, and TRUTH, all true Christians admire,
In the ABSTRACT at least—or till tried in the fire;
For the poor honest soul with suspicion they scan,
And consider him rather a " *strange sort of man.*"

But Divine Compensation! when cometh thy day!
Man's cloak of "respect" shall be rent in dismay;
'Tis a fearful mistake, 'tis a terrible plan,
To be nought but a " Highly Respectable Man."

THE WEE SPUNK LADDIE.

—page 75.

THE WEE SPUNK LADDIE.

LANGSYNE a wee wean used to come to our door,
  His claes were aye dirty an' duddie ;
His feetie were blacken'd wi' mony a score,
  An' we ca'd him the Wee Spunk Laddie.

He'd stan' at the door wi' the spunks i' his lap,
  An' a bunch i' his wee bit han'ie ;
My mither wad gie his bit headie a clap,
  An' ca' him "her wee bit mannie !"

Aye blate was his look when his piecie he gat,
  An' ance we speert whaur was his daddie ;
Sae red grew his cheek an' sae little he spak,—
  We were wae for the Wee Spunk Laddie.

An' aye we jealoused he fear'd to gang hame
  When fardens were few in his neevie,
For sair wad the wee laddie greet by his lane,
  An' sab owre his wee droukit sleevie.

Whan Willie wad bogle at Doddy's aul' coat,
  My mither wad fleetch the bit laddie ;
Belyve, she wad tell him, just " never to mind,
  She wad gie't to the Wee Spunk Laddie."

Whan ane his bit luggie o' milk wadna hane,
   An' leave owre a sowp o' his crowdie;
Oh, he was ca'd "thankless" and "wasterfu' wean,"
   That sud think o' the Wee Spunk Laddie.

But she kiss'd us a' roun', and the tear gather'd big,
   Whan she heard a' aboot our bit plannie,
To put our bawbees in the aul' pirrlie pig,
   To buy claes to the Wee Spunk Laddie.

An' oh, whan we took the bit wean to the kirk,
   Sae fear'd like he took his bit placie;
We wish'd a guid wish frae the core o' our heart,
   As we watch'd his bit shilpit facie.

An' aye he cam back, an' his wistfu' bit look
   Wad counsell'd the thochtless an' gaudy;
For He that aye kens what the helpless maun brook,
   Was guidin' the Wee Spunk Laddie.

Noo the puir bodies' frien', wha's braw shop's his ain,
   Wi' the sign o' the Gowden Caddie,
Was ance a bit waefu', dung-donnert-like wean,
   For *he ance was the Wee Spunk Laddie.*

THE LOSS OF THE *HERON*.*

LIKE white-winged Hope her gay canvas was swell'd,
For a glorious purpose the *Heron* impell'd ;
O, her mission of mercy ennobled her crew,
And a hero's heart beat 'neath each jacket of blue,—

To strike off the chain from poor Africa's son,
(The trophy a Christian church should have won) ;
O it was not for gold that she sped o'er the wave,
But to stay the man-stealer and rescue the slave.

When hell-charter'd slavers were skulking from view,
Like light o'er the luminous waters she flew ;
'Twas death to the cruel, the fleet, and the strong,
When she closed with the ruthless Goliath of wrong.

There were shouts, there were cheers, there was rushing
        below,
To cargoes of souls—to the children of woe ;
There were tears of humanity shed by the brave,
And they mingled with those of the brother and slave.

Though tears on the earth, they are gems in the sky,
For angels sublimed them and bore them on high,

* Her Majesty's sloop of war, the *Heron*, Captain Truscott, lost on
the coast of Africa. She had bravely captured four slavers with heavy
"cargoes," shortly before she was struck by the tornado.

Weep not for thy Henry !* weep not for him now,
Like a halo they gleam on his beautiful brow.

The *Heron* has finish'd her holy career,
And ne'er struck her flag to a foe or a fear ;
The appalling TORNADO shriek'd over the wave,
And she sank like a Howard while seeking to save.

O saintly abettor ! O priest of the free !
Her story is censure *conniver* to thee ;
He is false to his God, from the poop to the stem,
He whose heart is not true to the children of men.

———o———

TO A YOUNG LADY ON HER MARRIAGE-DAY.

MYSTERIOUS tie, which binds the heart to home,
That draws so tight whene'er we have to roam,
The starting tears will from thy heart of truth
Pay Nature's tribute to the home of youth.
And yet, while parting thoughts your bosom wring,
You'll yet more fondly to your husband cling,—
Heaven bless you both !
   May ye each other prize,
And build unfading treasures in the skies,

* A handsome young officer much regretted.

That in your hearts may glow the sacred charm,
Which takes the sting from every earthly harm ;
Which makes, with angel grace, the Christian wife
Point towards heaven, and smooth the path of life !
Now may your hearts, like dewdrops in the sun,
Be fill'd with light, and mingle into one,—
That holy light by Truth's great spirit given,
Which thrills, exalts, and lights the soul to heaven.
More wishes rise than we have time to tell,
But Heaven shall hear our prayers—
       Farewell ! farewell !

————o————

I'LL NO DO'T AGAIN.

WHAN the wee bit tot lassie has pyket the scone,
Or fylet the bit frockie she's new gotten on,
If she's ca'd doon a dish, or stay'd out i' the rain,
She sabs to her mither, " I'll no do't again,"
       " I'll no do't again,"
       " I'll no do't again."

Whan the wee laddie's taen doon the watch frae
    the wa',
An' hurtit the hannies sae bricht an' sae sma' ;
If he's taen out the razor that's lippin'd to nane,
He cries when he's cloutit, " I'll no do't again !"
       " I'll no do't again !"
       " I'll no do't again !"

If he has stay'd frae the schule, or been tellin' a lee,
If he's lost his bit buik, or has stown a bawbee;
If he's broken a window, an' fear't to gang hame,
The wee heartie's sichin, " I'll no do't again,"
                     " I'll no do't again,"
                     " I'll no do't again."

O wonderfu' words! they are aye on the tongue
O' saunt an' o' sinner, o' auld an' o' young;
They've a power that wad saf'en the heart o' a stane,—
They words o' contrition, " I'll no do't again,"
                     " I'll no do't again,"
                     " I'll no do't again."

O frail human heart! though in purpose upricht,
It forgets, like the wean, whan he's out o' yer sicht;
Whan its virtues at last o' its follies think shame,
The soul sichs in sorrow, " I'll no do't again,"
                     " I'll no do't again,"
                     " I'll no do't again."

THE SCENTED VIOLET.

I LOVE the flowers! their balmy breath
    Subdues the troubled soul to rest;
But though I fondly love them all,
    I love the Scented Violet best.

Sweet flower! though fairer forms I see
    In bright and beauteous colours dress'd,
And glorious though their beauty be,
    I love thee, Scented Violet, best.

Thy home is oft the cultured spot,
    But though it be the tufted grass,
Thou ever smilest on thy lot,
    Nor is thy balmy sweetness less.

Though crush'd beneath the proud one's tread,
    True greatness doth thy soul express;
A richer fragrance dost thou shed,
    And sacred seems the lowly grass.

Then ne'er may hardships, though severe,
    The incense of the soul suppress;
Let love adorn our lowly sphere,
    Nor let our gratitude be less.

K

RISE, O MY SOUL.

RISE, O my soul, in gratitude to God,
　Whose mercy raised me from a bed of pain;
Cling to the arm His endless love extends,
　And breathe thy praises in a humble strain.

Lord, 'tis Thy mercy sheds the sunny ray,
　Thy love directs and mingles with the storm;
So pain is oft the harbinger of love,
　And danger, love's most salutary form.

For it doth whisper tidings to the soul
　No voice can utter and no tongue express;
Reason, half conscious, startles at the sound,
　Nor vainly tries to stiffle or suppress.

For then it is that spirit speaks with spirit—
　And spirit hath a language of its own—
At once the sage and savage understand
　Its thrilling voice and its electric tone.

Then sinks the host of metaphysic lore,
　Its strongholds perish and its guardians fly;
Reason exalting, 'mid dispersing clouds,
　To nobler purpose strains her eagle eye.

THE WEE LADDIE'S GRIEF.

—page 88.

For all that's mortal then looks back to home,
   Bearing towards its native earth again;
But thou, O spirit! hear'st a Father's voice,
   And look'st to the Great Source from whence ye came.

Touchstone of Truth! when I must follow thee,
   Whose very shadow makes delusion fly,
May Faith and Hope resign me to thy arms,
   And Love give wings to bear me to the sky!

——o——

THE WEE LADDIE'S GRIEF.

I GRAT upon my mammy's bed,
   I frichtit grew, an' sairer grat;
I cried upon her owre an' owre,
   But aye she lay an' never spak.

I tried to gar my mammy speak,
   But aye folk cam an' push'd me back;
I cried upon her owre an' owre,
   But aye she lay an' never spak.

They wadna let me kiss her cheek,
   Her hand they wadna let me tak;
I cried upon her owre an' owre,
   But aye she lay an' never spak.

At length they said she was awa,
  An' gied me things I cudna tak ;
An' aye they tell'd me no to greet,
  An' said that mammy wad come back.

Hoo glad I'll be when mammy comes,
  Hoo sune her roun' the neck I'll tak ;
I'll tell her hoo her Willie watch'd
  An' wearied for her comin' back.

She used to haud me to her breast,
  An' on my broo big tears wad drap ;
Although she lay an' didna speak,
  I'm *sure* that mammy'll come back.

———o———

HOW SMILING HER CHEEK.

How smiling her cheek, there's the sunshine of heart,
That gladdens the soul ere its treasures depart ;
In fancy she meets him—she falls on his breast,
And she breathes not for joy while in fancy caress'd.

Oh, joyous wife ! soon the blackness of night
Shall startle thy soul from its dream of delight—
The *Chieftain* approaches—she touches the shore—
But—the arms of thy sailor shall clasp thee no more.

He sleeps in the deeps of the turbulent tomb,
That waits not the waning of pride and of bloom ;
The transport of joy, by thy fancy impress'd,
Is the last that thy day-dream shall build on his breast.

Weep ! weep ! and let none dare the tears to restrain,
Those waters that cool the dread fires of the brain ;
The heart of affection, when agony fills,—
They're the balsam the Angel of Mercy distills.

Weep ! weep ! till thy Father, the "guide of thy youth,"
Shall trouble the soul-healing waters of truth ;
The " still small voice" over thy spirit shall steal,
With the peace that the soul-stricken only can feel ;—

The peace that this valley of tears cannot give,
The peace that all changes of earth shall outlive,
The peace that shall tell, when thou heavest the sigh,
Of the home where thy "Hasser"* shall meet thee on high.

* A young Swede, named Hasser Matteson, who fell from the rigging
of the *Chieftain* of Kirkcaldy, and was drowned, when but a short dis-
tance from the home where he was hourly expected by his young wife.

THE PROCESSION.

PROV. xx. 11; xxix. 17.

THEY come! the sound of music nears,
The hopeful band of tender years;
They come with merry flute and drum,
With smiles of joy they come! they come!
A tide of beauty meets the view,
With floral gifts of richest hue;
They pass, they pass, and it is sweet
The glance of youthful joy to meet
From hearts that cannot yet conceal
The bliss-like happiness they feel;
It gladdens like a sunny ray,
And childish joys long pass'd away,
Once more athwart the spirit gleam,
And whisper what we all have been;
Fair flowers adorn each tiny hand,—
They pass, they pass, the happy band!

But see yon mother's fond delight,
Her little daughter comes in sight,
And she is fair to look upon;
Ah! more than fair, she is her OWN,
Her blushing bud of beauty mild,
Her world of joy, her only child!

And see yon father's honest pride,
His sons are passing side by side;

He smiles, their smiles of love to see,—
A happy, happy man is he.
He feels no power on earth could part
The ties that bind them to his heart;
He prays that grace their steps may guide,
And murmurs blessings on their head.

Yon mother, too, with bright'ning eye,
She sees her darling boy draw nigh;
Thoughts rise which tongue could never speak,
She longs to pat his dimpling cheek.
Her bosom heaves, she knows not why,
And tears—yes, tears—bedim her eye;
Through silent drops of love and joy
Her eye still lingers on her boy—
They pass, they pass, to music sweet,
A stream of pleasure fills the street!
But see yon shrunk and aged form,
The clay, but not the soul is worn;
Her eye dilates, her treasure nears,
The nursling of her stricken years;
He sees not yet that she is nigh,—
She marks his fond expecting eye.
At length their looks in rapture meet,
And tardy grow his little feet,
And pride and love his bosom share,—
" He knew that granny would be there."

They pass, they pass,—on, on they wind,
And soon they leave the town behind;

We follow fast, we cannot stay,
To bonnie Raith* we must away.
The grey-hair'd portress comes in state,
And open flings the peaceful gate ;
They enter in, their spirits bound,
They lightly tread the fairy ground.
The sheep forget the daisy green,
And gaze in wonder on the scene ;
The bending boughs that kiss the grass
Seem fain to touch them as they pass.
In blue and silver of the skies,
"*The lake*" in passive beauty lies
Like some bright eye we've gazed upon,
Which shed no passion of its own ;
No inward tumult stirs its breast,
But lovely is its dreamy rest.
They reach the wide expanded green,
And sportful grows the festive scene;
The dance begins, the joyous dance,
And see yon blushing maid advance :
She smiles and blushes more and more,
For she has never danced before ;
And yet no diamond could outvie
The little maiden's laughing eye.

But evening comes by slow degrees,
And parting sunbeams bronze the trees ;
The joyous band their steps retrace,
And homeward turns each smiling face,

* The seat of Colonel Ferguson, Fifeshire.

While Evening fondly o'er them hings,
And fans them with her airy wings.

But now has ceased the flute and drum,
And now the parting scene has come ;
In happy groups they melt away
To tell the pleasures of the day.
Soon will a thousand tongues relate
The endless story of the fête ;
And some with rosy dimpled cheek,
And locks so wavy soft and sleek,
May call to mind, when old and grey,
The bright and long-remember'd day.
Thus guileless pleasures ever cease,
They dawn with joy and close with peace ;
Sweet while they last, they're sweetly true,
And bright in retrospective view.
O 'tis a happy sight to see
Youth's fearless joy and guileless glee !
No rules conventional have they,
They know not Pride's tyrannic sway :
Equal in rank, when so in joy,
No fear of change their dreams destroy,—
How *real* the gladness of the boy !

But when the Future shades the view,
The sight has sadness in it too ;
For well we know the coming years
Will bring them trials, and toils, and tears ;
And fatal sometimes is the strife,
When strange new passions burst to life.
L

Some strive for wealth, some rise to fame,
And some may sink in sin and shame ;
Some sleep beneath the briny wave,—
Some live to fill a pauper's grave.

But, parents, much on you depends
Which way the yielding sapling bends ;
When love to thee his young lips move,
O tell him of the Saviour's love !
Thou art the stem his love must twine,
As medium to a love divine ;
Then ere thy God-like reign expires,
O upward turn his young desires ;
Point the young fibres of his love
To Him whose reign is truth and love,—
To Him who gave his spirit birth ;
Nor let them grovel on the earth !

Your children's hearts were sweet and fair
When God first gave them to your care ;
If tares you sow in soil so sweet,
O never hope to gather wheat !
The fruitless barley of the wild
Is like the poor neglected child ;
Yet culture could have made it yield
The golden treasures of the field.

O blessed task ! O task how dear,
To guide, instruct, direct, and cheer !
The child a Father's love has given
To bless thy home, and nurse for Heaven.

"The world," you say, "will make him wise;"
Ah ! but at what a sacrifice !
In mercy think ! what bitter things—
What anguish—tardy wisdom brings !
The world's tuition !   Ah, how dear,
How cruel, how caustic, how severe !
When her cold words the truth impart,
She rudely smites the youthful heart,
And bitter are the tears of woe
That from the chasten'd bosom flow.
In wrath alone does she reprove,
She never, never schools in love ;
But oft hath driven—by wounds she gave—
To crime, to madness, and the grave !

Then till the heart, and watch with care
The seeds that sin hath hidden there ;
Be faithful to his infant years,
And pluck each weed as it appears ;
Believe no hand this earth upon
Will *pluck so gently as your* OWN.

Behold the floweret's gloomy fate,
That blooms *at last*, but blooms too late ;
Nursed by a cold, ungenial clime,
It knows no glorious summer time,
And quails beneath unkindly skies,
And cowers, and shrinks, and droops, and dies.

Then till the heart, and while you sow,
Pray God the increase to bestow ;

But, fear the ray of soul unsoil'd—'
The keen discernment of thy child.
Whate'er he hears you supplicate,
He knows the gift you would not take.
Strange light have children from the skies,—
They read the soul with angel eyes,—
They know whate'er the tongue may state,
Whate'er we love, whate'er we hate.
For *mercy's sake be true!* and know
Great is thy power for weal or woe.
He hears, but best He loves to SEE,—
A watcher of the hands is he ;
And builds his faith from day to day,
On what you DO,—not what you say.

————o————

DINNA DESPAIR.

In a' thing that grows there are creatures sae wee,
Ye've to look through a glass ere the wee things ye see ;
An' yet they're the life that gies vigour and birth
To a' thing that grows on the face o' the earth.

Then things are no trifles although they are sma',
An' naething's a trifle that can ye befa' ;
But the soul needs a glass as weel as the ee,
An' through faith we the wonders o' Providence see.

Although yer misfortunes surroun' like a flood,
Hae faith, an' ye'll see that its a' for yer guid ;
In shower, or in sunshine, there's Providence there,
Sae its duty to struggle, an' sin to despair.

Though nearest an' dearest on earth be untrue,
Be staunch to yersel, an' yer sure to come through ;
The warst frien' ye hae, and the warst to repel,
Is the merciless fae *ye can be to yersel.*

Then dinna despair whan yer frien's drap awa,
An' lichtlie yer name whan yer back's at the wa' ;
Be thankfu' ye *ken* ye can trust them nae mair,
An' try to forgie them—but dinna despair.

Though dark cluds like mountains sail through the
　　moonlicht,
As if they wad fain pit the moon out o' sicht—
Yet brichtlie she shines wi' her face to them a',
An' trusts to kind breezes to blaw them awa.

An' sae, whan the cluds o' misfortune draw near,
Oh ! aye let some hope be mix'd up wi' yer fear ;
For whiles they grow brichter the nearer they draw,
An' aften kind Providence airts them awa.

Though base anes abraid thee and wad thee defame,
An' joy owre their efforts to blacken thy name,
Look calmly to Heaven an' dinna despair,
For the wrangs that ye suffer are register'd there.

An' dinna resent! but in virtue benign,
Commit a' to Him wha says "Vengeance is mine;"
An' ne'er let the worthless thy bosom distress,
For *they aye doot the virtue they dinna possess.*

And, oh! if cauld Death has made silent thy hearth,
An' loosed a' the ties that e'er bound ye to earth,
Yet dinna despair although lanely ye be,
For there's just the mair waitin' a welcome to gie.

———o———

A FRAGMENT.

'MONG Highland hills where wildness reigns,
    And bursting cascades rush to view,
Where Nature's rudest footsteps press'd,
    Or wildest Fancy ever drew,—
My home be where the eagles fly,
And mountains peer the Northern sky.

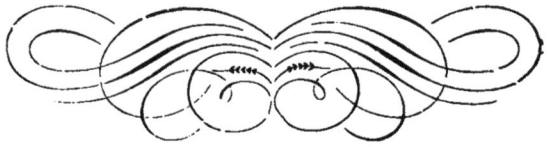

THE TWA GOWANS.

Twa wee gowans bloom'd on a gowanie lea,
Whaur a'thing was bonnie as bonnie cud be;
The ane had a tinge o' the red heather-bell,
An' the ither was white as the snawdrap itsel'.

The white ane was genty—was winsom' an' wee,
The red ane was braw as a gowan cud be;
An' couthie they grew frae they sprang to the licht,
Whan their hearties were young an' their headies
    were licht.

An' aye whan the wind wad blaw gurlie an' dour,
The red ane aye bent owre the genty bit flower;
Whan drappies o' rain on its breastie wad fa',
It tenderly lootit an' kiss'd them awa.

Whan aft-pitten breezes a daffin wud fa',
An' a' the braw floories wad touzle an' blaw,
The wee gowans joukit an' jinkit agee,
They boo'd an' they beck'd, an' waffled wi' glee.

But, ah! whan the red ane was ta'en frae the lea,
The wee ane lay doon on its divot to dee;
It lay in its beauty sae heedless o' a',
Like a wee drap o' gowd on a wee flake o' snaw.

For a' roun' the roots o' the floorie sae kind,
The white ane's wee threedies had long been entwined;
Their hearties were ane, an' they wadna be twa,
An' the bonnie wee floorie sune wither'd awa.

————o————

SINCERITY.

Though life her gayest scenes array,
And rosy gifts bestrew thy way,
'Tis but a sunless summer's day
Without the gem Sincerity.

When friendship youth's gay breast inspires,
Her warmest glow his bosom fires;
But soon the fitful flame expires
Without the gem Sincerity.

When first we love we fear no care,
Unconscious that a barb is there;
But when its pangs the bosom tear,
We sigh for sweet Sincerity.

A fiend may smile the lover's part,—
O fear the lips that praise impart;
Nor trust till thou hast found a heart
That shrines the gem Sincerity.

THE SEQUESTERED FLOWER.

— page 97.

Tho' Beauty, fair as mid-day light,
May boast of all that charms the sight ;
Her smile is dark as starless night,
Without the gem Sincerity.

————o————

THE SEQUESTERED FLOWER.

LET sorrow envy thee, sequester'd flower,
   Unknown to woe thou court'st the silent shade ;
Happy ! thou seem'st to throw neglect on all,
   To smile in peace beneath that glossy blade.

No care hath e'er disturb'd thy gentle form,
   Sweet flower ! *thy* paradise on earth was given
Bright, pure ; celestial gems bedew thy leaves,
   As Evening strews her precious gifts from Heaven.

Fair Morning hastes, impatient at thy tears,
   And softly warbles many a glad'ning sound ;
Then kissing all thy bright'ning tears away,
   Day's cheering sunbeams fondly smile around.

Ah ! once like thee, no surge Life's waters swell'd,
   For then my mother soften'd every wave ;
That bosom, ever true, as dawn to morn,
   Now sleeps with William in the silent grave.

M

O it is this that chills my weary breast,
  Nor can a mother's smile my hopes restore ;
Though tears for ever wash my sallow cheek,
  That brother's love can cheer this heart no more.

One earnest wish this aching heart retains ;
  May its fulfilment bronze my evening sky !
Shield me from frozen Pity's eye of death,
  Spare me the worldling's hideous sympathy

But, O Religion ! beacon of the soul !
  Thou only canst the time-toss'd spirit save ;
Thy voice alone can breathe the precious hope
  Of meeting those we love beyond the grave !

———o———

THE MANIAC.*

SHE comes again !
  Why does she come with sighs ?
Lydia !
  Why meet me now with pensive eyes ?
Why—when thy beauteous form I fly to clasp—
Why do you vanish, to elude my grasp ?
Those eyes again !

---

* Many years ago, at a ball in Edinburgh, a young lady received the
marked attention of a gay officer, to the no little pain of a young gentle-
man in the room, to whom she was betrothed. Proud and sensitive in
his nature, and roused by the jealousy allowed to be inseparable from

O why those looks of woe—
Why do you look to wound my spirit so?
'Tis painful, Lydia, thy grief to see;
But—death to feel thou hidest it from me.
Ha! now it comes!
      The thought that fires my breast
Comes fiercely on, and will not be suppress'd,
It smites my heart, it stabs and stabs again;
It comes like burning lava o'er my brain;
It comes! it speaks! it says that you regret
We ever loved, or that we ever met;
If so, fear not to tell me!   .
       Tell me now,
And soon the sorrow shall forsake thy brow;
Though seas of anguish o'er my spirit roll,
Know he who loves thee hath no paltry soul,—

strong affection, the youth, unable to control his emotion, demanded the officer to desist; who, in reply, struck him on the face. Furious with rage, he rushed at his tormentor to avenge the indignity; but the blow *never fell*—he was surrounded—the officer retired—peace was restored; but the earnest, loving, sensitive youth was a maniac, and remained so to the end of his days.

The image of her he so dearly loved, weeping in bitterness over the result of her thoughtless frivolity, remained upon his soul for ever. He was boarded at a decayed village, about seven miles south from Edinburgh; and as he wandered the woods and walks of the district, with his proud excited step, he constantly addressed her in the language of endearment or reproach.

Well do we remember his proud and elegant bearing; and as he passed us, muttering his fervid words, so evident and great was his occupation of fancy, that even the youngest of us experienced awe, and observed a respectful silence.

Know he who pledged thee in the sight of God,
Can spurn whate'er is grudgingly bestow'd.
Ha! now you weep!
   What *mean* thy tears and sighs?
(O hide this change mysterious from my eyes!)
I cannot bear thy grief,—but stay, O stay!
Why weep o'er love so *lightly thrown away?*

Now my soul wanders sadly o'er the past,—
Where did I see thee smile upon me *last?*
Ha, I remember!
   At the festive scene,
Where the dark spirit came our souls between!
 Why did you lean upon his arm and smile,
When my heart throbb'd with agony the while?
Why did they hold me when he struck the blow?
Why did they hurl me to yon dungeon low?
Yon awful darkness!
   Darker than the tomb,
Yon fearful midnight of unfathom'd gloom?
 Spare memory!—spare!
Withdraw thy maddening scroll,
I feel a fatal tempest in my soul :—

  O why do I wander,
   O why do I roam ;
  Ah, why do I love
   Thus to wander alone?
  Why gnaws in my bosom
   This festering pain ;

Why kindles my soul,
  And why smoulders my brain ?

She was fair as the sun,
  She seem'd kind as his beam ;
She smiled to deceive me,
  Yet true did she seem.

I was lull'd by the charms
  Which around me she threw ;
I kiss'd her base trammels
  As fonder I grew ;
Nor knew till delusion
  Had burst at my feet,
That her bosom was fraught
  With the basest deceit.

Why now does she come
  With her sorrowful eyes ?
Why follow me now
  Through the woods with her sighs ?
She whispers my name,
  As she whisper'd of yore,
But she meets me in tears,
  And with gladness no more !

MY FIRST-BORN.

She came to my soul like a sunbeam of bliss,
    Like a ray of God's gladd'ning light;
My fond spirit folded her under its wings,
    And I wept with a holy delight.

I gazed on her beauty, I heard her soft breath,
    With feelings I never had known—
I trembled with joy as I lovingly dreamt
    That the beautiful gem was my own.

A rapturous dream was that dream of my soul,
    Too bright and too blessed to stay;
Forgive me, O God! the wild moment of doubt,
    When the child of my love pass'd away.

Some griefs have a gloom, while they sadden the soul,
    A solace would seem to impart;
'Tis the veil the angels hang over the soul,
    While they bind up the wounds of the heart.

But O, there are wounds that they never bind up!
    In silence they let them bleed on;
They know that till death they can only be wash'd
    By the tears that are shed when alone.

Believe not, though smiles light the mother's **pale cheek**,
    One drop of her sorrow is gone ;
Ah, no ! every smile has its tribute to pay,
    In the tears that she sheds when alone.

They are sacred to truth—they are sacred to **Heaven**,
    And hopes that for ever have flown ;
They spring from the fathomless deeps of the **soul,**
    The tears that are shed when alone.

----o----

YER NEARER GOD, MY BAIRNIE !

YER nearer God, my bairnie !
    Than whan ye were wi' me ;
An' though we noo hae pairtit,
    Its only for a wee.

An' ilka nicht that I lie doon,
    Before I steek my ee,
My heart gies thanks that I hae come
    A day's march nearer thee.

Owre guid wert thou, my bairnie !
    Owre guid to bide wi' me ;
I only got ye, bairnie,
    To *haud* ye for a wee.

An' while I held ye to my heart,
  Sae dear wert thou to me,
I thocht if ye were askit back—
  My bairnie!—I wad dee.

I wearied for the sunny days,
  I wearied for them sair;
I watch'd the dreary winter cluds
  Wi' silent dread an' care.

Dark fears cam creepin' owre me,
  Whan cam the frost an' snaw;
But bitter, bitter woe was mine,
  Before they gaed awa.

'Twas awfu' sair, my bairnie,
  'Twas awfu' sair to pairt;
An' O its awfu' sair to live,
  An' hae a broken heart.

But safe are ye, my bairnie!
  The gentle heart o' thine
Will never, never ken the woe
  That wrings this heart o' mine.

The warld's noo dark, my bairnie,
  Its dark an' drear to me,
For gane is a' the happiness
  That I hae haen wi' thee.

Although I ken yer faulded safe,
  An' Wisdom says to me,
That "I sud gladly thole what's gien
  Sic happiness to thee,"—

It's ill to see through blindin' tears
  A truth sae sair to learn;
Fain, fain wad I hae keepit thee,
My bonnie, bonnie bairn!

———o———

BRUISED.

    LORD give me faith
      Thy love to know,
    Although my tears
      In anguish flow.
Fix Thou, O God, the blest belief,
Which yields the bleeding heart relief;
Assure me in this hour of pain
That I shall meet my child again.

    A fearful night,
      An awful gloom,
    Hangs o'er the drear
      And silent tomb.
And O the dark, the dire dismay,
To mark its merciless decay!
O give me faith, O give me power,
To trust thee in the midnight hour!

N

Lord, I believe!
But in my grief
Help Thou, O God,
Mine unbelief.
O may this poor weak heart of mine
Lean on the living words of Thine,
That pierce through Nature's deepest gloom,
When they arraign the silent tomb!

When Faith and Hope
Wax faint and low,
And tremble on
The floods of woe,—
O may my bruised spirit hear
Thy words—to human love so dear—
" Where now, O Death! where is thy sting,
And Grave! what trophy dost thou bring?"

My heart is weak,
My daily bread
Is moistened by
The tears I shed.
Lift up, O God! if it may be,
The veil that parts my child and me;
Assure me in this hour of pain,
That I shall meet my child again!

FOLLOWING FAST.

WE are following fast,
We are following fast,
   We are nearing the ghostly shore ;
As a breath upon glass
Fleeteth life as we pass
   To the ones that are gone before.

Let us dream as we may,
Life is only decay,
   A thing that fleets by like a breath ;
Ah ! the loved and the dear
May not sojourn here,
   All is touch'd by the finger of Death.

His dark shadowy wings
Hang o'er all treasured things,
   Over all that the spirit holds dear ;
When we dare to rejoice,
There's a small spirit voice
   Comes chilling the bosom with fear.

Though he breathes every breath
Under sentence of death,
  So wondrous a creature is man,
In his dream of an hour,
He is regal in power,
  Though it passeth away like a span.

For dominion hath he
O'er all creatures that be
  On the face of this beautiful earth;
And the Ancient of Days
Gave the sceptre he sways,
  When he first took him out of the earth.

O the reins of his power
He holds tight for an hour,
  And he rules with a resolute hand;
All Nature obeys
The proud sceptre he sways—
  The elements wait his command.

O he soars in his might
Through all vistas of light,
  And dares every mystery unfold,
From the lore of the skies
To the wisdom that lies
  Buried deep with the systems of old.

The dread lightnings that fly,
They in ambush must lie,
   Must listen for thought at its birth,
And come trembling to tell,
In the power of his spell,
   What's felt at the ends of the earth.

Where the tempest first sighs
They are lurking like spies,—
   O'er oceans they whisper " Prepare ;"
And to him they reveal
All the secrets they steal
   From the deep, and the clouds of the air.

E'en the sunbeams at play
Come with smiles to obey
   His tender and loving behest ;
And the pictures they leave
Seem to live and to breathe
   When the loved ones have long been at rest.

Such is man in his might,
When he drinks with delight
   The cup by proud Science distill'd !
Ere the footfalls of woe,
Coming silent and slow,
   With terror his bosom has thrill'd.

O the roses are rife
In the morning of life ;
    But many who gather their blooms,
Ere the close of the day,
Wound themselves in dismay,
    And wander unclothed 'mong the tombs.

There's a network most fair,
Most wondrous and rare,
    O'er the hearts of us all at our birth ;
But some fine fibre tears,
With each pang the heart bears,
    And is ne'er reunited on earth.

It is found ever fair,
Without rupture or tear,
    On the heart of the newly born ;
But at death it is seen
Ravell'd up like a skien
    That's rudely been twisted and torn.

O a beautiful earth
Is this place of our birth ;
    But its joys, like the mirage, depart ;
O for all we love best,
It hath no place of rest,
    And deeply it woundeth the heart.

Like the streamers that fly
O'er the dark Northern sky,
   Are the glimpses of human delight ;
O they brightly draw nigh,
But like phantoms they fly,
   When the soul would fain bathe in their light.

There's a strength to endure,
There's a trust—*O how sure !*
   Before sorrow the bosom has wrung,
That fainteth and fails,
When the anguish assails,
   And the cords of the heart are unstrung.

While there's joy at the heart
It is easy to part
   With all we may love to pursue ;
We can bear for the strife
And do battle with life,
   Nor murmur the strife to renew.

Let all treasures depart
But the *ones of the heart,*—
   Let the sunshine of love but remain,—
Every toil has a charm,
We can brave every harm,
   And brave it again and again.

Though the tear-drops may start
While there's joy at the heart,
   Its brightness they cannot conceal;
For the thin clouds that fly
O'er the bright summer sky
   The sunbeams more brightly reveal.

O it lights up the eye
Like a star in the sky,
   And strengthens the reins of the heart;
Till cometh the gloom that o'ershadows the
     tomb,
   We know it will never depart.

But when fond hopes are crush'd,
And loved footsteps are hush'd,
   And our joys pass away like a scroll;
When Death and dismay
Chase our sunshine away,
   And darkness broods over the soul;—

Then the feeble knees yield
On the dark battle-field,
   And the spirit would fain be at rest;
Too weak for its strife
The soul sickens at life,
   Fallacious and febrile at best.

Nothing true can it give ;
We but dream while we live ;
   But when the Eternal we find,
Truth cometh to slay,
For, when dreams pass away,
   We are naked, and feeble, and blind.

Then the winepress of woe,
That no flesh can forego,
   We must tread all alike and alone ;
Death must yet agonise,
For this mortal that dies,
   Immortality yet must put on.

We are following fast,
We are following fast,
   Separation will soon be o'er ;
When the loved ones again
To our bosoms we'll strain,
   And joy we are dreaming no more.

Then the child of our love,
Like a white-winged dove,
   Shall leave us again no more ;
But shall nestle and rest,
And remain to be press'd,
   To our bosom for evermore !

AUNTIE.

O AUNTIE, woman ! kind and true !
Weel may I bathe yer bonnie broo ;
Weel may I watch the hale nicht through,
    Wi' loving care,
Weel may I wait upou thee noo,
    Baith late an' air.

I'll smooth a pillow for thy heid,
I'll pit mair happin ou thy feet,
An' rub them, till they come a-heat,
    An' cozie be ;
I'll steer the fire, an' syne I'll weet
    The pickle tea.

I'll pit a pillow at thy back—
The wee drap "jute" fu' guid I'll mak,
An' coax ye till yer cup ye tak,
    Yer spunk to raise ;
An' syne ye'll gie's a wee bit crack
    O' bygane days.

A drowie thing I used to be,
An' meikle toil ye've haen wi' me ;
For nichts ye wadna steek yer ee,
    But watch wad keep,
An' dawt me, till I garr'd ye dree
    I'd fa'n asleep.

But out at a wee corner slee,
I used to keek wi' pawkie ee,
An' see thee laigh to Him on hie
    Thy speerit bow,
An' beg for blessin's rife to be
    On my wee pow.

An' ae that this puir heart o' mine
"Micht never pree the pangs o' thine !"
An' sair perplex'd was my bit min',
    Whan tears I saw ;
But—Auntie !—
    I hae learn'd sin syne
    What garr'd them fa'.

THE STRICKEN TREE.

It was not frail!—its spreading boughs
   Gave pledge of greatness yet to be ;
We dreamt that many yet unborn
   Would love our fondly-nurtured tree.

It was not frail ! its leafy charms
   Were gay in youth's own gladsome green ;
And yet we thought a mystic sigh
   Would come its merry songs between.

Ay, Stricken Tree ! we've watch'd thy form,
   When sad-like stillness o'er thee fell,
And thought thy listening soul was stirr'd
   With feelings that thou couldst not tell.

Oh, Stricken Tree !—so fresh, so fair,
   So soon to break beneath the blast,—
Thou stirrest in thy grassy lair
   The wakeful spirit of the Past.

WILLIE AND 'TINA.*

WILLIE! with the angel eye,
Gone! and yet for ever nigh—
Now I hear thee tell thy name—
Now I steal thy "turls" again;
Willie! thou art with me ever,
Thou shalt leave my spirit—*never*.

Hear me tell "the story" o'er,
Look as child ne'er look'd before;
Ask me what I cannot tell—
Hold my spirit in thy spell;
Cradled on my soul for ever,
Thou shalt leave my spirit—*never*.

Now wee "Tina Toddle Ben!"
Now I guide thy steps again;
"Auntie's bastit" now you see,
Ah! there's something there for thee;
Lift the lid, with pawky look,
Catch the bonnie picture book.

* Children of G. L. D. M'Intosh, St Andrews, and the much beloved niece and nephew of the Author.

Toddle to thy mammy's knee,
Sigh again her tears to see ;
Now your " noonie! noonie ! " say,
Try to wipe her tears away ;
Children ! ye are with me ever,
Ye shall leave my spirit—*never*.

Children of eternal day !
None shall tempt your steps to stray ;
Free from sin, and free from sorrow,
Ye shall fear no dark to-morrow ;
Time shall wound you never, never,—
Ye are safe, and save for ever.

None shall leave ye ! none shall grieve ye !
Ne'er, O ne'er ! shall Death bereave ye !
Ne'er shall grief your bosoms pain,
Ne'er shall sin your spirits stain ;
Time shall wound ye never, never,—
Ye are safe, and *safe for ever*.

SONGS.

MY JAMIE AN' ME.

Though Fortune should bear him,
Or Fate rudely tear him,
   Awa to the farest-aff isles o' the sea ;
Our sauls wadna sever,
Never—ah, never,—
   We'd aye be thegether, my Jamie an' me.

Time's fading and fleeting,
Its love's but a greeting,
   But ours is a love that has never to dee ;
Naething can break the ties
Twined in eternal skies,
   An' naething can sever my Jamie an' me.

Ours is nae love o' earth,
Pure is its place o' birth,
   Ours is a love that was cradled on hie ;
Calm as a dreamy cloud,
Bright as a starry shroud,
   Deep —deeper by far than the deeps o' the sea.

Nought can divide us,
The ties that unite us
   Were spun by the fingers o' angels on hie ;
We are thegether
For ever and ever,
   O Death canna sever my Jamie an' me !

P

I'VE BASK'D IN WORLDLY SMILES.

I'VE bask'd in worldly smiles, my girl,
   In Fortune's sunny day;
But when the hour of darkness came,
   Bright eyes were turn'd away.

But like the starry light, my girl,
   Thy love knows no decay;
When dark the hour, more glorious
   Its bright and holy ray.

I will not call thee fair, my girl,
   Such praise shall ne'er be mine;
I know the beauty of thy soul,—
   Let others praise the shrine.

A spirit-love is thine, my girl;
   The soul that blends with thine,
Dwells but on earth, but lives for Heaven,
   Thou guiding star of mine!

MY MITHER'S AULD.

My mither's auld an' unco frail,
　An' dim has grown her ee ;
Her doitit looks gang to my heart—
　I canna gang wi' thee.

O think when I sae helpless lay,
　A wee thing on her knee ;
For a' that's guid below the lift,
　Wad she forsaken me ?

O David loed his Absolom,
　Baith deep an' tenderlie ;
An' he had ither weans to loe,
　But she has *nane but me.*

Were we to pairt, nae mair on earth
　We'd ane anither see—
I canna, canna break the heart
　I ken wad break for me.

The young may pairt, and hope to meet,
　In spite o' land or sea ;
But Hope's a bud that canna bloom
　Upon a stricken tree.

The wintry blast alane sud strip
  The cleedin frae the tree ;
Sae I sall be my mither's beild,
  Till Death pairt her an' me.

———o———

IT'S NO THE GENTLE AIR SHE BEARS.

It's no the gentle air she bears,
  Its no her broo sae fair an' sleek,
It's no the witchin' air she wears,
  That's touch'd my brain an' blanch'd my cheek.

She told me that her heart " was mine,"
  Ae spirit-life we seem'd to share ;
I thocht her saul was roun' me twined—
  I thocht her mine for ever mair.

Ere a' the licht o' life had fled,
  Hope thus her tale wad whisper me :
" The stars, sae constant to the heavens,
  Aft twinkle oot o' sicht a wee."

But she was like yon siller clud,
  That looks sae fix'd an' laith to gae,
An' only waits the passin' breeze,
  To waft it proudly on its way.

HE PU'D ME A ROSE.

page 125.

Hush, hush, ye thochts, ye weary thochts!
  Ye'll gar this wretched bosom thaw;
An' weel ye ken nae frien' hae I
  To wipe the bitter tears awa.

Come faithfu' Death! thy peace impart,
  Thou solace true for every pain;
Come, gentle healer of the heart,
  Come, balmy balsam of the brain!

———o———

HE PU'D ME A ROSE.

He pu'd me a rose bloomin' laich in the brake,
And said, "Dearest lassie, keep this for my sake;
I hae nae braw breast-preen nor gowd ring to gie,
But dinna forget me, though lowly I be."

At thochts o' "forgettin'," my heart gaed awa,
The tear fill'd my ee, but was frichted to fa';
He squeezed aye my han'—an' he look'd sae at me—
I grat, an' the tears fell like pease frae my ee.

That rose is a treasure I'll keep evermair,
I aye tak it out when my heart's awfu' sair;
But aye gin I look on't the tear blin's my ee,
An' ilkie bit leafie grows dearer to me.

O aye when I meddled my heart gies a pu',
As something had moved it, I dinna ken hoo;
A waefu' thocht speers gin he's aye true to me,
An' waters its leaf wi' the tear o' my ee.

———o———

THE HUNGARIAN GIRL'S SONG.

WE parted in silence, no word did we speak,
The eye became steadfast, and pale grew the cheek;
      A love that's immortal,
      What mortal can tell?
We parted in silence, nor breathed a farewell;
      Nor breathed a farewell,
      Nor breathed a farewell,
We parted in silence, nor breathed a farewell!

Though seas now between thee and Hungary roll,
Electric as thought is the converse of soul;
      Though Fate rudely stretches
      Her empire of sea,
Thy fond spirit tells me you're thinking of me,
      You're thinking of me,
      You're thinking of me,
Thy fond spirit tells me you're thinking of me!

In scenes of misfortune, of sorrow, and care,
I lean on thy spirit, I feel thou art there ;
    While calmly I smile on
    The tyrant's decree,
Thy fond spirit tells me you're thinking of me,
    You're thinking of me,
    You're thinking of me,
Thy fond spirit tells me you're thinking of me !

O weep not for me when my soul takes its flight,
For Death can but closer our spirits unite ;
    I'll hang o'er thy couch
    When thy soul's to be free,
I'll soothe thee and whisper, " I'm waiting for thee,
    I'm waiting for thee,
    I'm waiting for thee,"
I'll soothe thee and whisper, "I'm waiting for thee !"

————o————

THE DEAN.

O DEEP sinks the dew-drap that fa's to the floorie,
   That's dowie when a' ither floories are green ;
O deep sinks the drap o' the saft fa'in' shoorie,
   An' deep sinks affection where sorrow has been.

Tho' dark cluds again hover owre me in sadness,—
   O dear is the spot where the sunshine has been ;
Dear ilka step we hae stray'd in our gladness,
   Dear ilka leafie that grows i' the Dean.

O there the wee floorie,* sae dear to affection,
   Keeks lovingly up frae its divot o' green,
An' breathes a fond wish between hope and dejection,
   While tenderness dwells in its bonnie blue een.

Though half o' their beauty the lang grass encloses,
   They hide their wee headies, sae sweer to be seen;
They're dearer to me than the brichtest o' roses,
   The bonnie wee floories that bloom i' the Dean.

O there the wee burnie, sae laich an' sae loesome,
   It sichs like affection that daurna be seen,
It glints like the lowe that lies laich in my bosom,—
   The bonnie wee burnie that breathes through the Dean.

———o———

WHAN BUDS HAD SPREAD.

Whan buds had spread their dainty leaves,
   As if they never were to fa';
When gowans whiten'd a' the braes,
   An' clad them owre wi' simmer snaw,—

We met, an' O our tears were sweet
   As thae on Nature's bonnie face!
Whan April meets her sister May,
   An' tears bespeak their fond embrace.

        * The blue Forget-me-not.

INZIEVAR HOUSE.

—page 129.

O what are kingdoms to a queen,
  If love's a sweet she's no to pree?
Her croon it lacks the fairest gem,
  The licht that love alane can gie.

Let ladies gems an' rubies prize,
  For pearls let them rake the sea;
Mine be the gem—the peerless gem—
  That sparkles in my Jamie's ee!

———o———

THE BONNIE HOOSE O' INZIEVAR.*

AMANG yon wuds that kiss the cluds,
  Yon warblin' wudlands spreadin' far,
See! cuddlin' 'mang the openin' buds,
  The Bonnie Hoose o' Inzievar.
    The Bonnie Hoose o' Inzievar,
    The Bonnie Hoose o' Inzievar,
  See! cuddlin' 'mang the openin' buds,
    The Bonnie Hoose o' Inzievar.

The windin' Forth, that guards the North,
  Looks lovin'ly at Inzievar;
An' aye wi' pride, her swellin' tide,
  Sings, "Scaith yon blossom if ye daur!"
    The Bonnie Hoose o' Inzievar,
    The Bonnie Hoose o' Inzievar,
  An' aye wi' pride, her swellin' tide,
    Sings, "Scaith yon blossom if ye daur!"

* Country-seat of A. V. Smith Sligo, Esq.

Q

Half smoor'd in green, if e'er ye've seen
  The queen o' flowers keek like a star,
Out frae her veil o' mossy green,
  Ye've seen the Hoose o' Inzievar.
    The Bonnie Hoose o' Inzievar,
    The Bonnie Hoose o' Inzievar ;
  Then hae ye seen, half smoor'd in green,
    The Bonnie Hoose o' Inzievar.

The laverock's sang, the lift alang,
  Comes trem'lin' to us frae afar ;
But safter lays fa' frae a lip
  That sweetly smiles at Inzievar.
    The Bonnie Hoose o' Inzievar,
    The Bonnie Hoose o' Inzievar ;
  On ilka side, may weel betide
    The Bonnie Hoose o' Inzievar !

JOTTINGS.

JOTTINGS FROM SINCERITY'S NOTE-BOOK.

Ance I dwalt wi' a queen,
   A bonnie young queen,
An' spak i' the licht
   O' her bricht blue een ;
An' they lichted aye on the comely mien
    O' a knicht frae my ain countrie,
       My ain countrie,
       My ain countrie,
    O' a knicht frae my ain countrie.

But a' her proud frien's
   Spak lichtly o' me,
They said I belang'd
   To a laigh degree ;
An' they sent the braw knicht far owre the sea,
    The braw knicht frae my ain countrie,
       My ain countrie,
       My ain countrie,
    The knicht frae my ain countrie.

∴ But I wrung her heart
    Ere I gaed awa,
An' I garr'd her greet
    In her kingly ha' ;
An' I fled wi' the tear she last loot fa'
      For the knicht frae my ain countrie,
        My ain countrie,
        My ain countrie,
    For the knicht frae my ain countrie.

An' syne I fell in
    Wi' a braw young chield,
His haffits were fresh
    As a floorie field ;
He open'd his breast to gie me a bield,
      An' he took me his jo to see,
        His jo to see,
        His jo to see,
    His genty young jo to see.

But never wad I
    Let him ca' her fair,
Nor praise up her een,
    Nor her gowden hair ;
But I garr'd his heart grow heavy wi' care,
      An' as leal as a heart cud be,
        As heart cud be,
        As heart cud be,
    As leal as a heart cud be.

An' I garr'd the red—
  Red—flee frae his cheek,
An' his lowin' heart
  Loud an' wildly beat ;
An' geyzen'd his tongue whan he tried to speak ;
    Nae pawkie palavers had he,
        Had he—had he—
        Na, nane had he,
    Nae lang palavers had he.

But Wealth gied him waughts
  O' the war'ly wine,
(Aye the bitterest,
  Blackest, fae o' mine) ;
Sae he boasted me frae his bosom syne,
    An' fu' glib i' the tongue got he,
        The tongue got he,
        The tongue got he,
    Oh ! glib i' the tongue got he.

An' he praised her een,
  An' he praised her hair,
An' he praised her aye
  Till her *heart was sair ;*
An' plichted anither no half sae fair,
    An' he leugh in his sleeve at me,
        His sleeve at me,
        Wi' sneerin' ee,
    He leugh in his sleeve at me.

Syne I cam to the ha'
  O' a wide domain,
Whar Beauty's lips breathed
  Wi' rapture my name;
"I hae fa'n," quoth I, "'mong folk o' my ain,
    Among folk that are sib to me,
      Are sib to me,
      Are sib to me,
    'Mang folk that are sib to me."

But my bashfu' heid
  Fu' quickly I hung,
For fremmit was I
  To auld an' to young;
An' I fled wi' a heart richt sairly stung
    Wi' the looks they cuist at me,
      They cuist at me,
      They cuist at me,
    The looks that they cuist at me.

O I lichted syne
  In a merchant's ha',
A' thing was blythsome,
  An' a' thing was braw;
I sune was at hame an' liked by a',
    An' fu' couthie they dealt wi' me,
      They dealt wi' me,
      They dealt wi' me,
    Fu' couthie they dealt wi' me.

But, ah! whan I gaed
  To his countin' room,
He said, wi' a glow'r,
  A glunch, an' a gloom,
"At hame wi' the wife an' weans ye hae room,
    But BUSINESS is BUSINESS," quoth he!
        "BUSINESS," quoth he,
        "BUSINESS," quoth he,
     "BUSINESS is BUSINESS," quoth he!

Sae I fled! an' fell in
  Wi' a factory squire,
But, "I was a *han'*
  He didna require;"
His face turn'd black as he growl'd in ire,
    "Trade canna be trammell'd wi thee!"
        "For trade," quoth he,
        "Is *trade*," quoth he,
    "An' canna be tied wi' thee."

O I weared syne
  For a peacefu' hame,
An' I socht oot ane
  Wi' a sauntly name;
But his heart was cauld as the cauld whun-stane,
    Nae bowels o' compassion* had he,
        "Na,—na,"—quoth he,
        Wi' sauntly ee,
    "Religion's Religion," quoth he.
        * James i. 27.

R

But soun' were his views,
　An' his faith was bricht ;
" Faith's a' that can save,"
　He preach'd day an' nicht !
An' as for himsel, I thoucht he was richt,
　　For never by warks* wad it be,—
　　　　　" Na,—na,"—quoth he,
　　　　　　Wi' sauntly ee,
　　　" Religion's *Religion*," quoth he.

Sae I turn'd awa'
　Frae the cantin' hame,
Whar Faith was stark deid—
　Religion a *name*—
An' thocht I wad gang to auld Poortith's hame,
　　For he aye can coont kin wi' me,
　　　　　Coont kin wi' me,
　　　　　Coont kin wi' me,
　　His aye kith an' kin to me.

But ere I got there
　My heart gied a sten,
I'd landed mysel
　In a critic's den,
Whar they slauchter'd folk wi' strokes o' the pen;
　　And O ! losh-'ave-a-care-o'-me,
　　　　　A-care-o'-me,
　　　　　A-care-o'-me,
　　O ! losh-'ave-a-care-o'-me !
　　　* James ii. 14-20.

He clouted my lugs,
 An' he nevell'd me weel,
He ca'd me ill names,
 An' spak o' the wheel ;
I dwaum'd when he dookit the pointed steel,
 An' the dread fireflaucht i' his ee,—
   His dreadfu' ee,
   His dreadfu' ee,
  The dread fireflaucht in his ee !

Whan breathin' cam back,
 I was flichter'd an sair,
Till I REALLY saw
 Wha sat i' the chair ;
An' *the auld leein' loon Ananias was there,*
 An' for him I cared nae a flee,—
   An' sae ye see,
   An' sae ye see,
  Folk sudna be flichter'd wi' a' that they see,
   Wi' a' that they see,
   Wi' a' that they see,
  We sudna be flichter'd wi' a' that we see!

CPSIA information can be obtained
at www.ICGtesting.com
Printed in the USA
LVHW011519210220
647795LV00012B/627